PROTESTANT STRATEGIES IN EDUCATION

# Monographs in Christian Education

## C. ELLIS NELSON, *Editor*

---

No. 1  Protestant Strategies in Education

ROBERT W. LYNN

No. 2  Education in the New Testament

IAN A. MUIRHEAD

No. 3  Learning in Theological Perspective

CHARLES R. STINNETTE, JR.

# PROTESTANT STRATEGIES IN EDUCATION

by Robert W. Lynn

ASSOCIATION PRESS, NEW YORK

*Publisher's stock number: 1559*
*Library of Congress catalog card number: 64-20241*

PRINTED IN THE UNITED STATES OF AMERICA

# ACKNOWLEDGMENTS

In writing this monograph, I have often been reminded of how much I owe to other companions along the way. Some of the passages in the first two chapters are drawn from my doctoral dissertation, *Family-Sunday School Partnership: A Chapter in the History of Protestant Educational Strategy,* presented to the faculty of Union Theological Seminary of New York City in 1962. In that connection I am glad to acknowledge the following contributions of others: the generous co-operation of Montview Boulevard Presbyterian Church of Denver, Colorado (and, in particular, the thoughtfulness of the Reverend Arthur L. Miller and the lively help of Mrs. George H. Curfman, Jr.); the United Presbyterian Church for the honor of being a Presbyterian Graduate Fellow in 1959; the judicious criticism and sustaining presence of my colleagues and mentors of those years—Professors Robert T. Handy, C. Ellis Nelson, and Robert McAfee Brown.

During the work on this essay I have relied greatly upon the guidance of Professor Nelson and the encouragement of Professor Handy. They have given much, though I would not claim their approval for all that is set forth here. Likewise, I am grateful for the competent assistance of Miss Anne R. Walline of Auburn Theological Seminary in New York City and also of Mrs. Joseph E. Stetson of North Leeds, Maine.

A few paragraphs of this monograph are taken from my

essay, "The Making of an American," *The Search for Identity: Essays on the American Character* (New York: The Institute for Religious and Social Studies, distributed by Harper & Row, Publishers, Inc., 1964). I am grateful to the Institute for permission to use this material.

The author's thanks are due also to the following publishers for the use of brief extracts from their works as indicated in the Notes for the chapters: Basic Books, Inc., Columbia University Press, Dell Books, Harper & Row, Publishers, Inc., Horizon Press, Inc., The Macmillan Company, Meridian Press, Inc., Pilgrim Press, Princeton University Press, Random House, Inc., and Charles Scribner's Sons; and to the following periodicals: *Christianity and Crisis, The Commonweal, The New Republic, The Reporter,* and *Religious Education.*

Finally, as a token of love, I dedicate this essay to my father and mother—William McGregor Lynn and Janet Reid Lynn (1889-1964).

# INTRODUCTION

Protestant strategy in education is in a state of crisis, and part of the crisis is the Protestant's lack of awareness of major shifts that have taken place in our society.

Before the Civil War the policy of separating the church from the state in the control of public schools was developed; and, although some denominations and a few individuals saw that this decision would secularize education, they were unable to make any effective countermoves.

After the Civil War, Protestants were content to rely on their dominant position in the nation and the enthusiastic promotion of the Sunday school, youth organizations, and later the Vacation Bible School, reading and teaching Bible in public schools and other agencies for religious education.

Soon after World War II, the Supreme Court in a series of decisions took the view that religion should be separated from the schools; and this view culminated in their decision in June, 1963, that a devotional reading of the Bible and a recitation of the Lord's Prayer were unconstitutional. This latter decision brought to an end all arrangements that used the public schools to support or promulgate any religious belief. Released-time and shared-time programs are still legal, but these are arrangements of school time for religious instruction on a voluntary basis and do not commit the public school to anything.

What shall Protestants do now that public education is officially secular? Shall we put our energy and money in shared time or some other effort to provide religious instruction adjacent to public schools? Should we abandon our traditional support of public education and establish parochial schools? Can we expect a new Moses to lead us into the promised land where religion informs and reforms education? No one knows the best course of action for our nation and our faith, but we must first do what Dr. Robert Lynn proposes in this monograph. We must become clear about the conditions in our immediate past that have created our present situation, and then we must start a long search for a new strategy.

Dr. Lynn's careful study will give us the perspective and understanding we need for this crisis, and his method of analysis in the last chapter may point to a new Protestant strategy.

—C. ELLIS NELSON
Editor, Monographs in Christian Education

# CONTENTS

*Introduction* by C. Ellis Nelson      7

*Preface: Prelude to a Larger Task*      11

1. THE MAKING OF A COMMITMENT      13

2. CONTINUITY AND CHANGE      27

3. A NEW OCCASION      51

4. SOME UNFINISHED BUSINESS      74

# Preface:

## *Prelude to a Larger Task*

In the spring of 1964 the publication of a modest tract *Are Parochial Schools the Answer?* * [1] created a lively stir across the country. Much of the controversy revolved around Mary Perkins Ryan's negative answer to her question. Yet the ensuing conflict has obscured the significance of this little book. It is important, not because of any solutions offered, but rather as a contribution to the task of historical self-understanding.

Mrs. Ryan's primary intent, as I understand it, is to free American Catholicism from the burden of a dead past. That burden is evident in the so-called Catholic educational ideal —every Catholic child in a Catholic school. Both this ideal and the parochial school system are products of a "siege mentality," [2] the defensive response of the church in a pan-Protestant culture. Now the siege is over, she says, and so Catholics stand at the beginning of a different era. Though few Catholics are ready to dismantle the system of parochial schools, many are aware that a period of history is ending and a new occasion in American education is coming into sight. [3]

And what is happening on the Protestant side? For the most part, main-line Protestantism seems to be busily engaged in giving advice to the Catholics—such as adopting shared

* Numbered notes for the Preface and all chapters appear at the end of the book.

11

time, not asking for governmental aid for parochial schools. Yet we, too, are burdened by our immediate past, although perhaps in a less obvious way than the Catholic community.

My aim in this monograph is to aid Protestants in understanding the *presentness of the past* as it is expressed in the "typical Protestant parallelism of public school and Sunday school." [4] I shall trace the career of this commitment in the opening chapters. This thought-form, developed in mid-nineteenth-century America, has continued to inform much of our thinking about education. It has undergone minor modifications, to be sure; but, on the whole, Protestants have clung to it despite massive alterations of the American scene. The shift in underlying circumstances has not yet been properly recognized and accepted. An analysis of this strand of events is offered out of the conviction that "an unexamined history operates in us as fate." [5]

These reflections on the past and present will only hint at the full complexity of the problem before us. Make no mistake about it. In the American setting the question—how does our form of Christian education relate to the offerings of the public school?—is not just one among many possible social action issues that might occur to the alert Christian. On this educational scene, that is the question *par excellence* about the relation of faith and culture. With rare exceptions, it has not received serious attention from historians and theologians. What follows here is a preliminary report, an initial attempt to mark out some ways of exploring the history of Protestant educational strategy. [6] Hopefully, this monograph will encourage others to join the author in a further correction and clarification of these provisional observations.

It is, in sum, a prelude to a larger task.

# 1 THE MAKING OF A COMMITMENT

The sociologist, Louis Wirth, once observed that "the most important thing . . . that we can know about a man is what he takes for granted, and the most elemental and important facts about a society are those that are seldom debated and generally regarded as settled." [1] This dictum, now something of a sociological truism, is still an apt warning, for that which is taken for granted is often invisible. We can therefore be doubly attentive when an interpreter comes along and identifies one of these important facts.

James Hastings Nichols has done just that in the following observation:

> In the most general terms, American Protestantism for the last four generations has supported a dual system of education. The same generation before the Civil War built up parallel institutions, the American public school and the Sunday school, designed to educate children in secular and religious subjects respectively. . . .
>
> From the beginning there have been Protestants who have questioned the wisdom of this policy, but the Protestant community as a whole has supported it and still does.[2]

In this compact summary Nichols sets forth the major presupposition of Protestant educational strategy. But what is the meaning of this elemental fact? How did American Protestants arrive at the dual system of education? And what has the pattern signified to each succeeding generation? These are the questions that I propose to answer in these first two chapters.

## An Article of Faith

Our story begins in a turn of events around the middle decades of the nineteenth century. During those years—from the disestablishment of the last vestige of the colonial state-church system (1833) to the Civil War—Protestant education underwent a quiet transformation. The consequences of that transformation are with us yet.

Prior to disestablishment, church education rested upon a triangular institutional base: congregation, home, and school. It was the responsibility of the congregation to provide catechetical instruction and of parents to teach their children both the Scriptures and the catechism, and of the schools (such as they were) [3] to assist in this enterprise as well as instruct the young in their letters and heritage. Such interlocking cooperation seemed to be a natural working arrangement, an ideal [4] intended though not always realized.

By the end of the Civil War, the ideal of the triangle had been set aside. It could no longer serve as the normative arrangement for American Protestantism. Out of these middle decades came two suggested revisions of strategy: (1) A minority of Protestants advocated a system of parochial schools [5] as a means of combating the apparent "secularization" of the emergent public schools. In time, however, this movement faded away as ineffective rear-guard resistance against the "nonsectarian" school. (2) The majority had become irrevocably committed to the dual pattern, "this typical Protestant parallelism of public school and Sunday school. . . ." [6]

## At First, a Reluctant Embrace

This "parallelism" came to be "typical" through a unique confluence of historical circumstances. It is important to recall these circumstances, lest we unwittingly make over these nineteenth-century Protestants in the current image. They did not set out to create the dual system in the self-consciously rational, deliberate manner of the twentieth-century church "planner." (In this respect the retrospective application of contemporary categories of thought—such as "educational strategy"—is potentially misleading.) Rather, they accepted it, once it was established, as the likeliest arrangement for their time and place.

There was, for example, more ambivalence and hesitation in the Protestant *rapprochement* with public education than our present proprietary sentiments about the schools would allow us to acknowledge. The Protestant churchmen of the "national period"—like so many of their fellow countrymen—were caught up willy-nilly in the drive toward reform and expansion of the American schools. A blend of idealism and self-interest propelled them along a path that their forefathers could not have anticipated and that, as a matter of fact, they did not always welcome or relish.

First, the element of idealism. The reformers in their midst were quick to point out the fraudulent inadequacies of the existing systems. From the "tireless pen" of Horace Mann in Massachusetts, says one historian, ". . . came the whole dreadful story of sectarianism, incompetent teachers, inadequate supervision, primordial schoolhouses, dilapidated equipment and so on to the low standards and lack of uniformity." [7] Other crusaders, such as Henry Barnard of Connecticut and Rhode Island, joined in Mann's plea for a universal tax-supported education. What was needed, they argued, exceeds the scope of any private humanitarian venture. The new schools of the Republic must be common—open to all, free for all.

Only that kind of common school, built upon public control and support, could fit the new generations for the arduous tasks of nation building. "It may be," Horace Mann declared, "an easy thing to make a Republic; but it is a very laborious thing to make Republicans; and woe to the Republic that rests upon no better foundation than ignorance, selfishness, and passion." [8]

Second, the appeal to economic and political interests of a most diverse sort. Not all of Mann's peers shared his robust confidence in public education. Yet they were often fearful about the disruptive effects of "ignorance" and "passion," particularly in a new nation where every white male citizen over twenty-one years of age had access to the ballot. The reformers were aware of these apprehensions and so advocated the public school as a potential preventive of or remedy for many social ills: the perils of illiteracy, anarchy, and mob violence against property rights; the curse of poverty and restricted opportunity for the working man. [9]

For native-born Protestants perhaps the most persuasive argument of all concerned the school as the answer to the fundamental problem of this young country—the maintenance of a sense of corporate identity. Note the cultural anxiety implicit in this representative plea on behalf of Protestant-sponsored colleges in the Midwest:

> Another peculiar demand for colleges may be found in the immense rapidity of our growth, and in the character of that growth, being the representative of almost every clime, opinion, sect, language and social institute, not only of this country but of Christian Europe. Never was a more intense power of intellectual and moral fusion requisite to prevent the utter disorganization of the society. Never was a people put to such a perilous proof of its power of assimilation, or required to incorporate within itself so rapidly such vast masses. [10]

Much the same appeal was used in developing support for the public schools. Here, the reformers claimed, was America's best hope in this "laborious thing" of making Americans.

These considerations accurately reflected the emergence of a new situation and its demands. Thus, in the middle decades a majority of Protestants (represented alike among the educational reformers and their audience) found themselves moving toward a twofold recognition: first, they acknowledged (sometimes begrudgingly) the necessity and legitimacy of the public school; by the same token these Protestants were forced to admit the inability of the churches to meet this enormous challenge out of their own resources. As Sidney Mead has said, ". . . the task was too immense to be supported by voluntary churches that claimed as members only 10 or 20 per cent of the total population. And so somewhat by default the state took over what had traditionally been part of the work of the church." [11]

But, one might argue in retrospect, why did not the Protestant churches seek state subsidy for their own system of schools? Such an approach was tried in New York City during this transitional period—and with instructive results!

In the early 1800's the Free School Society (and its successor in 1826, the Public School Society) was backed by state funds in its efforts to provide free "nonsectarian" schooling for the children of New York City. It was, in contemporary terms,[12] an illustration of the blending of "public" and "private" resources: a philanthropic society, broadly Protestant in leadership and motivation, depended upon state subsidy to carry out its humanitarian program. This venture into "public" education was challenged intermittently during the 1820's and 1830's. The Roman Catholics, in particular, were alienated by the Protestant flavor of these free schools; consequently, they sought state aid for the establishment of their own schools.

Finally in 1840 William H. Seward, Governor of New York State, in a move to rectify this injustice, proposed that the state legislature subsidize the Catholic parochial schools in the same manner. That possibility quickly aroused Protestant fears and nativistic animosities. The controversy around Seward's plan precipitated the creation of a different pattern. The state legislature cut off its prior support of the Public School Society and, in its place, established a city board of education with the power of developing a new school system. And many of the Protestants, faced with an uncomfortable choice, preferred the lesser of two apparent evils. Rather than allow state funds to go to Roman Catholic schools, they chose instead to support the option of what seemed to be—at least from their vantage point—a more "secular" school. Such was the logic that drove some Protestant churchmen toward a newfound commitment to public education.

The same logic prevailed in the matter of religious instruction in the public schools. Here the difficulty resided in both the Roman Catholic-Protestant tension and also in the persistent in-fighting among Protestant denominations over "nonsectarian" teaching.

The story of Roman Catholic opposition to Bible reading in the public schools during the nineteenth century is well known, and we need not linger over it. In Philadelphia, New York, and elsewhere, Catholic spokesmen objected to the use of the "Protestant" Bible (the King James version) in the classroom. The Protestants of the national period were mystified and angered by these displays of seeming intransigence. So Horace Bushnell, a renowned Connecticut minister, wrote in 1853:

> In most of our American communities, especially those which are older and more homogeneous, we have no difficulty in retaining the Bible in the schools and doing everything necessary to a sound Christian training. Nor, in the larger cities, and the more recent settlements, where the population is partly Roman Catholic, is there any, the least difficulty in arranging a plan so as to yield the accommodation they need, if only there were a real disposition on both sides to have the arrangement. And precisely here, I suspect, is the main difficulty. There may have been a want of consideration sometimes manifested on the Protestant

side. . . . But there is a much greater difficulty, I fear, and more invincible, on the other side.[13]

That hoped-for accommodation was, of course, not forthcoming. But then neither was much accommodation between the Protestant denominations on the issue of "nonsectarian" religious instruction. If anything, Bushnell underestimated the difficulty of a Protestant agreement on "doing everything necessary to a sound Christian training" in the public schools.[14] For ". . . it was soon discovered," Sidney Mead comments, ". . . that there could be no 'nonsectarian' religious teaching in America, because religion had been poured into sectarian molds and had hardened in sectarian forms. Thus Horace Mann's brand seemed to many evangelical Protestants to be suspiciously 'Unitarian,' and at best what passed as 'nonsectarian' religious teaching seemed to many Unitarians, Roman Catholics, and others to be evangelical Protestantism." [15] And thus the Protestant denominations—each fearing the Roman Catholics, but also distrusting one another—became committed to a school that was more secular than they would have otherwise desired.

Yet one must be chary in using the word "secular" when describing the public schools of midnineteenth-century America. This word has taken on a distinctively new meaning in recent years. It would be a mistake to claim that the school of one hundred years ago was the same creature as the secular, de-religionized institution so ardently sought now by some Protestant theologians and others in the twentieth century.

With characteristic force—and exaggeration—Will Herberg says of these schools, "The public schools to which Catholic parents were required to send their children in the latter half of the nineteenth century were, to all intents and purposes, Protestant schools, claiming to be 'nonsectarian' because they were nondenominational within Protestantism." [16] That is close to the truth. The nascent public schools, although increasingly forbidden to engage in explicit religious instruction, were nevertheless often staffed by Protestant teachers and inevitably influenced by the Protestant ethos. In agrarian America, where the evangelical spirit was strong, that was surely the case. But, even in the cities, the centers of a growing Roman Catholic population, the Protestant influence was still pervasive—so pervasive, in fact, that a Catholic teacher was often barred from employment in public schools. In these situations the Protestants enjoyed a decisive advantage and an apparent security.

## A Common Task

Finally, they were reassured by the apparent devotion of some schoolmen to the task of moral education in the public schools. On this score Horace Mann—to cite the obvious example—was most convincing. Here, as perhaps nowhere else, the great reformer both reflected and shaped the American embrace of education.

In commenting upon the past, Mann said of the Puritans: "Two divine ideas fill their great hearts: their duty to God and to posterity. For the one they built the church; for the other they opened the school. Religion and knowledge, two attributes of the same and glorious truth, and that truth, the only one on which immortal happiness can be securely founded." [17] Probably this interpretation tells us more about Mann than about the Puritans. In characteristic fashion he mated religion and knowledge: a volitional religion in which the *will* of God and man is decisive (shades of Puritanism) and moral knowledge of the demands of society and of conscience. The offspring of this marriage was *moral education*.

In his estimate, mankind's capacity for anarchy makes moral education a "primal necessity." "The unrestrained passions of men are not only homicidal but suicidal; and a community without a conscience would soon extinguish itself." [18] But mankind's capacity for education makes this enterprise a great possibility. Mann was fond of the proverb, "Train up a child in the way he should go, and when he is old he will not depart from it." [19] And so he was profoundly hopeful about the possibilities of moral education—the training of the child's will so that he will move naturally and consistently toward the good. "Education has never yet been brought to bear with one hundredth part of its potential force . . . upon the character of men. . . ." [20] The "way" toward the good was self-evident (though not, in Mann's version of it, cheaply realized); the supreme task and opportunity of the public school was moral education.

Moral education, thus interpreted, has informed much of our thinking about the nature of education—whether in the public or in the church school. This tradition was powerfully present in the minds of those nineteenth-century Protestants who came to trust the parallelism. The avowed purpose of the Sunday school movement was more explicitly evangelical. Its founders envisioned a larger task, as we shall shortly see. Yet the making of the moral man, if not the Sunday school's *raison d'être,* was nevertheless an anticipated consequence of its existence. In this way the work of moral education became a common denominator, a point of convergence in the respective purposes of two parallel institutions. The seeming naturalness of this marriage of social functions eased the way toward the acceptance of the public schools.

These were, in brief, the circumstances that shaped the Protestant commitment to the public schools during those formative decades in the nineteenth century. Out of this tangle of considerations has come a pattern of thinking, a characteristic mixture of "yes" and "no" that prevails with some modification to this day. Of course there has been a continuing opposition to any diversion of public funds toward Roman Catholic schools; indeed, among many churchmen in the main-line denominations, this "no" has been extended to negate even the possibility of Protestant parochial schools. At the same time, the "yes" toward public education has generally become more uncritical and absolute. In the intervening years Protestant churchmen tended to forget the original hesitancy of some of their forefathers in accepting public education. The cultural hegemony of Protestantism and an ensuing sense of dominance in school affairs—these are some of the factors that have propelled Protestants toward a complete embrace of the cause of public education. What had been, in the beginning, a matter of social necessity and a way of keeping the civil peace was transformed in later years into a matter of belief, an article of faith in the unofficial but operative credo of American Protestantism.

## An Evangelical Movement

A fever of enthusiasm for the Sunday school ran high throughout American Protestantism during the middle and latter part of the nineteenth century. Today—when the Sunday school is often treated as symbolic of thin faith, a simplistic understanding of the world, that is, a "Sunday school faith," a "Sunday school morality"— it is difficult to comprehend the popularity of this institution just one hundred years ago. Yet such an understanding is necessary if we are to penetrate into the original meaning and vitality of the dual system.

Little is known about the earlier history of the Sunday school. It first appeared in eighteenth-century England as a one-day-a-week school for impoverished children. During the 1780's and 1790's and into the first decades of the nineteenth century a few of these "pauper schools" sprang up in America. As in England, the first American Sunday schools offered instruction in the catechisms and letters, a needed though drastically limited form of free schooling. Gradually, however, as the public schools became permanent, the Sunday school was converted into the major institutional form of Protestant church education. And, in that process, a multitude of Protestants became converted to the Sunday school and its promise.

For these Protestants the primary appeal of the Sunday

school did not reside in its novelty as an educational enterprise. To be sure, they appreciated its modest advances in teaching materials and methods. Its emphasis upon a direct study of portions of Scripture seemed to be more acceptable to a pragmatically minded people than the older "question and answer" procedure of the catechisms.[21] But these improvements alone do not account for the popularity of the Sunday school in the last century.

## The Evangelical Impulse

The promise of this institution lay in its possibilities as an *evangelical movement*. The Sunday school was, first of all, an expression of the *evangelical* thrust of Protestantism, embodied in educational activity. Here was a distinctively new instrument of evangelism fit to take its place alongside the revival system of an older day. Indeed, some hoped it would displace the revival. Winthrop S. Hudson says of the years immediately following the Civil War: "The most promising alternative to revivalism as an evangelistic device for the recruitment of church members on the basis of sound Christian experience was the Sunday school." [22] But whether a supplement or alternative to the revival, it was governed by some of the same standards and expectations. In intent the "Bible school" with all its paraphernalia was more than a proving ground for youngsters with a penchant for "memory verses" and perfect attendance; its reach included and yet went beyond the enterprise of moral education. It was, at its best, a proving ground for the Spirit and the souls of men.

During these same years Horace Bushnell suggested another way beyond the revival system. He considered the conscious abandonment of children until they reached a "technical" experience of conversion to a "nurture . . . of despair," a perverse and impossible educational scheme.[23] At the time that he was writing *Christian Nurture,* he was not overly drawn to the possibilities of the Sunday school.[24] Rather, he urged his contemporaries to look upon the home as the primary focus of Christian education. As the church is an extended family,[25] so the life of the church family is an indispensable and particularly vivid expression of existence in the church.[26] It is in the home, in the organic unity of parent and child, that Christian education—and fruitful evangelism—becomes a possibility.[27] The Church is a school, albeit a particular kind of school with its own unique ethos.[28] In that school the parents are strategically and providentially placed to be the teachers of young.

Bushnell's thesis, however, never gained the allegiance of his fellow Protestants. Christian nurture and conversion in and through the family did not seem to be a likely replacement of the revival system; nor did this notion ever threaten the supremacy of the Sunday school in their affections and loyalties. Perhaps it was too genteel for some,[29] and for others, too radical an innovation in educational strategy. In any event, the Protestant churchmen of the middle and late nineteenth century were so involved in the sweep and power of the Sunday school movement that they did not pay much attention to Bushnell's suggestions.

## A Voluntary Association

The Sunday school was a *movement* on the American scale. As the century unfolded, the Sunday school "workers" developed an elaborate organization with associations on the county, state, and national level, and with national and international conventions. Throughout its life in the nineteenth century, this movement reflected the genius of the voluntary associations of that time.

Winthrop S. Hudson has suggested that the voluntary society became the focused expression of Protestant energy and vitality in nineteenth-century America. They organized, he observes, to promote ". . . a host of causes—missions, education, peace, temperance, Sabbath observance, tract distribution, [and] manual labor institutes." [30] The Sunday school bore many of the marks of these organizations: it depended mostly upon lay leadership and financing; it was often interdenominational in scope,[31] and there was the usual ambivalent relation of the voluntary society to the churches. (In many a parish there were two congregations—one of which went home after Sunday school was over!) [32]

Above all, the Sunday school, like other voluntary societies, was driven by a vision of the unlimited good to be gained through its efforts. According to some, this movement had already altered the destiny of Protestantism and, indeed, of America. In the Lyman Beecher lectures of 1888, H. Clay Trumbull ventured the following estimate of the Sunday school's role in history:

> In the latter third of the eighteenth century Bible-study and Bible teaching were a minor factor in the activities of the Christian Church and the tide of vital godliness was at a very low ebb on the shores of Christendom. In the latter third of the nineteenth century Bible-study and Bible teaching have a *prominence never before known in the world's history* and vital godliness is shown and felt in unprecedented potency in the life and progress of mankind. This change is due to God's blessing on the revival and expansion of the Bible-school as His chosen agency for the Christian evangelizing and training.[33]

Trumbull's account of the past is best understood as an anticipation of a lustrous future, a vision of what was to come. If this "agency for Christian evangelizing" had brought Protestantism to such a full tide of "vital godliness" in the last third of the nineteenth century, then how much more could be expected of it in the first third of the twentieth century? That hope nourished a movement. It enabled the Sunday school workers to answer their critics with astounding verve and aplomb; [34] it also helped to offset lingering doubts about the reliability of the public schools. So, by the turn of the century, the "typical Protestant parallelism" had become a natural, comfortable arrangement. Most Protestants were ready to defend it as the American way and the Protestant ideal. Secure and confident, they awaited the beginning of the "Christian century."

To later generations, unacquainted with the romance of the Sunday school in these early years, such a hope now seems quaint and foolishly naïve. Such are the insights arising out of the luxury of retrospective wisdom. But though present-day Protestants may feel far removed from the experience of their nineteenth-century fathers, they are not strangers to certain beliefs generated by those events of an earlier time: a "blank check" confidence in the public schools, a corresponding optimism about the adequacy of slender marginal efforts in church education (that is, the Sunday school), and a conviction that these parallel institutions, although under different auspices and bound by somewhat different curricular responsibilities, were still yoked together by a common concern for moral education. All these attitudes, when they are taken together, form a dominant perspective that has held sway over much of American Protestantism during the last one hundred years. The persistence of this outlook in the twentieth century amidst changing conditions, has been barely acknowledged— and much less understood.

# 2 CONTINUITY AND CHANGE

In 1903 an illustrious group of professors, college presidents, and church educators met in Chicago.[1] The occasion: the formation of an organization—the Religious Education Association. Their intent (as formulated two years later): "To inspire the educational forces of this country with the religious ideal; to inspire the religious forces of this country with the educational ideal. . . ."[2]

The launching of the Religious Education Association (REA) marked the beginning of the liberal [3] era in Protestant church education. Although ostensibly an interfaith venture, the REA was largely dominated in its first five decades by a handful of vigorous Protestant educators. Indeed, these same men—the names of George A. Coe and his "son in the faith," Harrison S. Elliott, spring immediately to mind [4]—shaped the thinking of several generations of church educators. Their point of view prevailed in some places; their students and disciples became seminary professors and manned posts in the educational bureaucracy of Protestantism. In the lives of a few the REA functioned as a "church," a determinative community of orientation to the world around them. But for nearly all the religious educators, its twofold aim represented the substance of their hopes, the mandate for a life's work.

The mood of the times was such—and the erosion of Protestant theology so advanced—that these liberal educators never did make much headway in inspiring ". . . the educational forces of this country with the religious ideal." They succeeded best in inspiring ". . . the religious forces . . . with the educational ideal." Or, perhaps more exactly stated, they helped to alert main-stream Protestantism to the educational ideal of the progressive movement in the American schools. In his brilliant history of progressivism in American education, Lawrence A. Cremin says: "The word *progressive* provides the clue to what it really was: the educational phase of American Progressivism writ large." [5] So also one can say of the religious education movement: here was another manifestation of American progressivism in the first part of the twentieth century.

This period did not prove to be the climactic era anticipated by H. Clay Trumbull and his contemporaries. But that was only partly the fault of the religious educators. In these years the liberals, together with a few of their later critics, represented the *"best"*—though clearly not the *"most"*—of Protestant church education. Therefore, in this chapter I shall trace the recent career of the parallelism by focusing upon its meaning to this small but significant band of persons.

## From Confidence to Depression

In the manner of their fellow progressives, the religious educators brought vitality and fresh perspective to the institutions that were the targets of reform. They quickly demonstrated that Protestant church education was in need of a transfusion of energy and new ideas.

Outwardly Protestant church education of the early decades seemed to be in good health. Adelaide Case has described the period from 1900 to 1917 as a time ". . . of spectacular development in Christian education." [6] Certainly it was a time of experimentation in educational strategy. During these years of "pre-war expansion," [7] the first daily vacation Bible school was started in Wisconsin, and weekday schools for church education began in Gary, Indiana.[8]

Yet there was an undertow of vague uneasiness evident in these moves toward new forms. The nineteenth-century leaders of the Sunday school had spoken and acted with confidence. Now, however, the "old-time" [9] enthusiasm was on the wane. A generation ago the Sunday school was judged to be a powerful instrument of education. Some of the new leaders were unsure of either its permanence or its adequacy.[10]

These signs were indicative of a deeper and more subtle alteration in mood and temper. Despite a marked growth in the membership of the Sunday schools,[11] evangelistic zeal was tapering off in many churches into the " 'service club' spirit." [12] The tide of evangelical energy was gradually receding, leaving here and there a floundering institution. Most of the nineteenth-century voluntary societies, now subject to a process of "evaporation," [13] were "going native" and becoming secular. (The movement of the YMCA during these years— from an earlier concern with urban evangelism toward becoming another community organization—illustrates the process of "evaporation" at work; other examples might be drawn from the Protestant social work agencies and settlement houses.)

In this situation the religious educators brought an educational self-consciousness to a movement that had not always been so oriented in its evangelical past: a new awareness of men like John Dewey and their potential contribution to church education; a sense of relevant standards for evaluating teaching methods and materials; and the need for developing a profession of religious educators.

Through all these emphases they pointed insistently to the practice and presence of the public schools. And no wonder. Public education was casting a growing shadow over the American landscape. In the mid-nineteenth century, when the dual pattern first became fixed, that shadow had not been so long. In 1870, for instance, only "57 per cent of American children . . . were enrolled in schools; by 1918 the figure had passed 75 per cent." [14] An education in the public schools of rural America was often a "hit or miss" affair; the rhythm of harvest and planting determined the school year.[15] So ". . . the average number of days attended was just under forty-five in 1870." [16] By 1918 the widening impact of industrialization was apparent; the average number of days was past ninety per year.[17] In this fast developing industrial-urban culture, the public schools were becoming more central to its life and so more visible than ever before.

The early liberals did not resent the larger presence of public education. Their attitude was rather one of respect and reverence for its past accomplishments and future possibilities. Of the past, one speaker at the first convention of the REA said:

> . . . It soon became evident that the new nation had a most interesting and important experiment on its hands. This was nothing less than the reconstruction of the Tower of Babel. Immigrants streamed in from every land, speaking all the tongues that sprang up from Babel's ruins, and out of them a homogeneous people had to be constructed. What was the agency to rely on to do the work? Not the church, manifestly, for every ship brought a new sect. So it must be the school, and so the school became "the symbol of an eternal unifying spirit." [18]

This representative interpretation (circa 1900) re-echoes some familiar refrains from an earlier time, that is, a disdain for the Old World (Babel), yet a fear of its lingering influence in the New World, and thus the overriding importance of the problem of unity-in-diversity. But note also the development of a theme which up until now had been largely implicit in Protestant writings: the school is symbolic of both our national unity and God's handiwork in history. As such it was a sacred cause, worthy of religious devotion.

The public school also symbolized a new and better future.

It had become a laboratory in which the educational ideals of the progressives were being tested and criticized. They compared the Sunday school of their time with the best of public education and found it wanting.

In the ensuing efforts at reform the religious educators presupposed the parallel arrangement. If anything, they were more emphatic and self-conscious about its significance than their predecessors in the nineteenth century. The making of moral men, once considered to be the happy by-product of evangelical commitment through the Sunday school, was now becoming—at least for some—the rightful first aim of religious education. Their purpose was to keep the church school abreast of the public school, improve the churches' contribution to the joint task of moral education, and thus preserve the integrity of the "parallelism."

Some of them accepted the Sunday school as an institutional form and sought to bring about changes within. A few, however, were not content with such a strategy of patch and repair. In their estimate the era of the Sunday school was over. A new form must be developed if church education was to become comparable with public education.

Our attention here is upon the experience of those who took the second path.

## The Price of Religious Liberty

One of their number was Walter S. Athearn, professor of religious education at Boston University and the author of the "Malden Plan." Today a relatively obscure figure,[19] Athearn is important in this account because of the "Malden Plan." And the plan itself is important only as it embodies one man's struggle to reinvigorate the " typical Protestant parallelism" of public and church school.

In the mode of his generation Athearn adopted the public school as a "referent" institution, a source of normative judgment about educational organization, the standards of teacher preparation, finance, and administration. But unlike some of his contemporaries, Athearn was willing to acknowledge that the church school and public school were silent competitors for the time and loyalty of the younger generation. He insisted that ". . . the schools and colleges are not the only educational agencies in the community. The churches, the art schools, the private teachers of music . . . are all educative agencies. . . . Personally I am not so much concerned with academic credits as I am with *a fair division of the child's time among the various educational agencies of the community.*" [20] Such a thwarting of the community's rights contributes to the decay of America as a "Christian democracy." "It is becoming increasingly evident," he said, "that we cannot maintain a Christian democracy unless we maintain a system of efficient Christian schools. The price of our religious liberty is the sum required for the building of a system of church schools which will parallel our system of public schools and be equally efficient." [21] The parallelism must be kept intact!

So Athearn appealed to American Protestantism to go beyond its prior reliance upon the Sunday school. He made his case for a revision of educational strategy in a simple, cogent way:

> No education is complete which ignores the religious element. The religious element cannot be furnished by our public school system. Utilize it and standardize it as you may, the Sunday session of the church school will not furnish an adequate religious education for our people. These three propositions, if accepted, force us to a fourth proposition, namely, the church must have a share of the week days for religious education.[22]

Athearn was very eager to make this "fourth proposition" a live option, not only for Protestants but also for the Catholics and the Jews.

In the ill-fated "Malden Plan," [23] he proposed the development of a community-wide program of ". . . weekday religious schools sharing the child's time with the public schools during the regular school year." [24] The essence of his plan was "shared time"—a concept that was to be rediscovered some forty years hence and hailed as a new idea by a generation that had never heard of him. Athearn was not the first to suggest something akin to shared time; he was, however, among the first to think through the dislocations and demands of such a scheme.

He would settle for nothing less than a first-rate system of weekday church schools, staffed by professionally trained teachers, and supervised by a community board of religious education. This board was to be made up of laymen representing diverse denominations and free from all "ecclesiastical control." [25]

Athearn relied exclusively upon the "community consciousness" [26] of a Christian democracy, a spirit of co-operation that would enable men to rise above their parochial divisions (both the division of church against church, and that of the public school against the churches). He had little sense of the church as a people of God called out to witness to the community. The tension was not so much between the Christian and civil community as it was *within* the civil community. The church-culture tension had evaporated, and Athearn could muster only a weak appeal for "community consciousness."

In his theological understanding of the church, Athearn was surely a man of his time. But along with others [27] he discerned some important signs of the times: "the price of our religious liberty" was a vigorous dual system; the Sunday school was becoming increasingly marginal to a public school undergoing rapid expansion and professionalization; there was no safety, then, in a nineteenth-century resolution of a problem that had taken on a new form and challenge in the twentieth century. In accepting that challenge, Athearn was ahead of his time.

*The Depressions: Religious and Economic*

For a while after World War I the drive toward weekday church schools gained momentum. These schools were of three varieties: (1) the "released-time" program was an arrangement whereby the public schools agreed to release one hour a week of the children's time to churches for religious instruction. This scheme was a "cut-down" version of shared time. (2) The shared-time scheme involved a more substantial division of the child's week between public and church school. In the "Malden Plan," for instance, a child might have spent a considerable portion of the regular school day away from the public schools. (3) The "after-school" program, as its name so obviously implies, was an autonomous enterprise, and consequently free from the difficulties of close co-operation with public school officials. For the most part the experimentally oriented educators of those years began with either an after-school or released-time program. In some instances these initial ventures were intended to be the "down payment" on a future development of shared time. But in almost all these experiments, they hoped to find a way beyond the Sunday school as Protestantism's *first* commitment in its educational strategy.[28]

The newfound interest in weekday church schools grew so swiftly that it caused alarm among observant leaders of the religious education movement. The most vivid warning came from George A. Coe in 1922:

> But the assumption that the whole movement [for weekday church schools] is really an advance seems to me to be dangerous . . . because I see alleged schools being started in great numbers upon a wrong basis, a basis so imperfect that there is bound to be a reaction. I foresee the possibility—I think I dare say the probability—of a slump so serious that the whole progressive movement in religious education will be checked. . . . I believe, however, that with religious consecration and conse-

cration to educational science, we can rescue the movement from its dangerous situation. . . ." [29]

Coe's characteristic appeals to "religious consecration" and "educational science" proved to be unavailing. The "weekday movement," growing all the while, continued its unprofessional and haphazard ways until the early 1930's.

Then the economic depression hit full force. And when it did, ". . . the weekday schools, as the latest efforts of the church, were the first to receive crippling financial cuts." [30] In fact, the whole religious education movement—still something of a relative newcomer to the life of American Protestantism—felt the whiplash of retrenchment; church school budgets were lopped, and directors of religious education were often the first to be fired.

Even more stinging were the complaints accompanying the economic reductions. The halcyon mood of the 1920's had disappeared and, in its place, was a growing predisposition on the part of churchmen to find fault with the religious educators. "It is probable," comments Herbert W. Schneider, "that the religious education program was 'oversold' and that the initial, intense enthusiasm for it naturally produced eventually a relaxation, if not reaction. The results hardly seemed to justify the elaborate institutions and the semi-professional effort." [31]

The beleaguered religious educators were subject to the same disenchantment. Some, indeed, succumbed to it. Among the disenchanted was E. L. Shaver, then working on the staff of the International Council of Religious Education. In the mid-1930's he was asked to contribute to a symposium on "How Effective Is Religious Education?" (a revealing question that was hauntingly popular during those days). His appraisal of the reformers' assaults upon an outmoded educational strategy was somber and searching:

The weekday religious education movement has had success in some quarters but it is not revealed as a universal remedy. The vacation school is doing a good piece of work, but it too does not give promise of adoption by the majority of the churches. Here and there the wish is expressed that the public school might teach religion, since (so it is implied) the church seems to be such a failure at it! None of these explorations in quest of some new organizational scheme seem to be prompted or aided in its [sic] development by a strong desire to meet the pressing social problems of today. They appear rather to be desperate attempts to preserve an institution which will do the thing it has been doing in the past. . . . Other agencies than the church seem to be doing more effectively the thing which the church at heart would like to do—to help persons achieve more abundant life.[32]

These words suggest the magnitude of the depression that now gripped the movement. It was fundamentally a "religious depression," [33] heightened by but not caused by the economic decline,[34] a slump with its own attendant terrors of bankruptcy and demoralization. I am not ready to estimate the extent of demoralization among the nonprofessionals, the mass of ministers and Sunday school workers across the country. But from a study of the REA journal, *Religious Education,* during the 1930's, I am convinced that Shaver's sense of failure was shared by some of his peers.

There was cause for bewilderment. In retrospect, the reformers' visions and labor had amounted to little. The similarity of ". . . the progressive movement in religious education" (Coe's phrase) and in the public schools was once a source of pride to church educators; now it prompted some to reflect upon the validity of their function and to wonder if, after all, religious education was really necessary. Was there anything distinctly Christian about their brand of moral education? Had the purposes of public and church education become so identical that there was no longer any palpable sense of distance between these two supposedly parallel institutions? Were the religious educators the unwitting agents of a process of evaporation, so that, under their tutelage, Protestant church education had "gone native" and become secular?

### New Directions, Partly Explored

The religious educators never did face up to the import of these covert questions. Nor did they ever recover their earlier confidence. For one thing, the succeeding years brought fresh troubles to an already troubled group. First, the Depression; and then, the unwelcome advent of a new theological climate of opinion.

In the early thirties the established leaders of the movement had studiously ignored (despite a few cogent warnings [35]) the distant rumblings of a theological revolution on the Continent. The "theology of crisis," they liked to think, was a momentary apparition, an ideological consequence of the dislocations of life in postwar Europe. Toward the end of the decade, as the theological warfare moved closer to these shores, the attitude of indifference hardened into a spirit of combative defensiveness. There were exceptions, to be sure, but the dominant religious educators became theological isolationists. Their response to the new theological challenge was a variation of the isolationist outlook in foreign policy: stress the differences between Europe and America and keep American religious life free to follow its own unique experience and destiny. Actually, the thrust of their argument was not so much against Europe as it was an expression of the longstanding, self-imposed isolation of the movement from the changing concerns of the churches.

Though defending the "faith of the fathers" (some of whom —such as Coe—were still very much alive) against all outsiders, the liberals did carry on an internal dialogue within their own ranks about the next step for religious education. Out of this discussion came several attempts to strike out in new directions.

### Religion and Public Education

One sign of change cropped up in the announcement of the theme for the REA's meeting in 1941. "For a great many years," reported the editor of *Religious Education,* "the Association had tried to infuse religious education with progressive educational methods." [36] He continued:

> Last year, however, we modified our emphasis. Instead of asking, what can education contribute to religion, we began to inquire, what can religion contribute to education. The increasing tendency to secularization can be countered only by an increasing effort at spiritualization.[37]

What such "an increasing effort at spiritualization" entailed remained undefined. But the large term—"secularization"—did refer to something specific. For the first time in the history of the movement, some religious educators were voicing a concern about the failure of the public schools to engage in religious instruction. Here, indeed, was a possible new line of action. Up until now, as Luther A. Weigle wrote,

> ". . . there has been a rather general disposition to accept the exclusion of religion from the public school as a matter of course, something closed and done, inevitable and irrevocable. Discussion of the problem has usually been more concerned with a rationalization of the present situation than with its serious reconsideration." [38]

Mr. Weigle, then Dean of Yale Divinity School and an "old-timer" in the religious education circles, along with F. Ernest Johnson, Harrison S. Elliott, and others, was determined to break out of that pattern of default. None of these men blamed the public school. (Its policies and performance were, significantly enough, exempted from Protestant critical analysis during these decades. I shall say more about this omission later on.) For the most part they reserved their fire for the church's complicity in this state of affairs—for the baneful legacy of nineteenth-century sectarianism [39] and the wholly unrealistic expectations of the Sunday school as a teaching instrument of the church.[40] Mr. Johnson, I believe, came even closer to the heart of the problem when he said:

The Protestant's attitude for a century has been dictated . . . by strategy rather than philosophical judgment. For underlying the Protestant position has been the rather naïve assumption that if the public schools could be protected from Catholic encroachment through drawing off funds for parochial schools or influencing school policies in other ways, the religious interests of the community would be well served. Until recently there has been little serious consideration in Protestant circles of the effects of secularism in education on religious attitude and outlook.[41]

Yet beyond an embryonic recognition of the problem and its sources, there was hardly any agreement about effective countermeasures. The weekday program of "released-time" instruction, now hampered by poor church support,[42] had as many critics as advocates.[43] Dean Weigle's proposal—"The common religious faith of the American people . . . may rightfully be assumed and find appropriate expression in the life and work of the public schools" [44]—never gained widespread support. The option most discussed by the religious educators in the late 1930's was the plan put forward by Mr. Johnson. He suggested that ". . . the same frank approach be made to a study of the churches [and religious beliefs] as is now made to the study of the industries, the press, the government, and the cultural activities of 'our town.' " [45] What is at stake in this matter, he claimed (and rightly, I believe), is not any supposed violation of the principle of separation of church and state but, instead, the educational integrity of the public school.

But even this third plan, modest in scope and happily free from constitutional questions, was subject to challenge. George A. Coe, for instance, remained consistently skeptical about its practicality. He said:

On the political side of our culture we practice free discussion as the way of "making up" our minds, and free discussion by pupils is practiced in the teaching of citizenship. The schools cannot teach religion in the same way because the religions have other methods of "making up" minds.[46]

And the churches, he intimated, would never tolerate any serious inquiry into their "authoritarian" procedures.

In the manner of his day Coe was sometimes indiscriminate in the way he branded his theological foes as "authoritarian." Yet, despite the polemical overtones of his analysis, he was probably correct in his reading of the cultural situation in the 1930's and 1940's. If the public schoolmen had engaged in a critical study of contemporary religious life during those years, they would have exposed themselves to reprisals and counter-attacks from all quarters.

Coe's own preference represented a fourth position. Instead of risking our hard-won cultural unity, he asked, why not encourage the public schools to teach democracy as a religion?

> Let loyalty to democracy be treated explicitly as religious. This is simple realism. There is an inherently religious quality in democracy when it is taken as a way of life and not merely as an institutional mechanism.[47]

Of all the options, Coe's was the least acceptable to the religious educators. Few of his colleagues were willing to go all the way with him. But his point of view was not altogether new or strange; it was, rather, a radically consistent expression of some of the movement's thinking in past years, as well as a possible reinterpretation of the nineteenth-century Protestant parallelism.

Let me explain how this is so. Coe looked upon society as divine:

> Society itself is primordial, and it is the ever-living source of energy that creates and re-creates the political order. The state, as an agent of society, does a part of the work of education. Parents do another part. . . . Similarly many voluntary organizations take part in both transmitting and modifying the ways of society that we call culture.[48]

He had no doubt that (in America, at least) the direction of society, that "ever-living source of energy," or—in religious terms—the will of God, was the progressive realization of democracy. Hence the truly religious task of the educator— whether in the public school, home, or church—was the making of the democratic man. Here, indeed, was the proper point of convergence of the purposes of public and church education. (Here also, as the reader will recognize, was the tradition of moral education in a somewhat modified form.) If Protestant church educators cannot join in this great adventure, then they should be willing to let the public school go ahead and fulfill its historic destiny. Coe's confidence in the public school was paralleled only by his growing distrust of the church school as a partner in this task. In his reliance upon the public school, one can discern a significant alteration of a prior attitude. In the nineteenth century many Protestants accepted the public school because it was often amenable to church influence; now, however, in the perspective of George A. Coe, the public school was acceptable precisely because it could transcend church influence. In sum, the public school had become the functional equivalent of the established church in the old order, in other words, the institution responsible for maintaining the unity and essential beliefs of a society.[49]

Coe, I think, would have heatedly denied that he was advocating anything so characteristic of the Old World as an established church. Unfortunately, the debate within the movement never did clarify this point. Although his fellow religious educators demurred from following his lead, they did not provide the grace of an effective opposition. The best challenge came from H. Shelton Smith, once an ardent participant in the movement and now increasingly its critic. After criticizing the world view of John Dewey and other experimentalists (including George A. Coe), Smith concluded his classic study, *Faith and Nurture*, with this prophecy:

> Thus the paramount question is this: What kind of religion shall the public school teach—the religion of the churches or the religion of humanistic experimentalism? Sooner or later this must

become the focal point of a crucial battle. On its outcome largely hangs the fate of democratic culture in America.[50]

The "crucial battle," however, did not take place in the following decades. Among the religious educators in the 1940's and 1950's, the discussion continued to be tepid and superficial. There were the usual pleas for bolstering released-time programs and/or teaching about religion in the public schools. But there was little willingness to dip down below the surface and dig out the deeper issues indicated in the opposing views of a Coe and a Smith. Is the public school the *de facto* "established church" of American society? Should it be? Can it be genuinely "secular" (whatever that chameleon word may mean)? What is the proper function of church education in relation to contemporary public education? These remained hidden problems, largely unexplored by either the religious educators or their successors of a different theological persuasion. And so the reconsideration of the nineteenth-century Protestant parallelism, now long overdue, was postponed for another day.

### The Partnership

Meanwhile, back on the "home front," there was an understandable anxiety about the limitations of the Sunday school. One way out, some religious educators believed, was to develop a genuine partnership of the family and the church school. This possibility was the second new direction taken in the latter part of the life of the movement.

The idea of an educational alliance between the Sunday school and the church home had been "in the air" for a long time. It had been intermittently discussed in the early decades of the century.[51] Then in the 1930's an increasing band of educators, still within the orbit of the religious education movement, commenced to stress the natural tie between the family and the Sunday school.

There were many reasons for the popularity of the partnership theme.[52] Its emergence at this time cannot be ascribed to the liberals' concern for a new kind of strategy. But their emphasis upon the alliance was a covert acknowledgment of the enfeebled state of the dual system of public and Sunday school, and a hopeful effort to strengthen it. In 1940 the writers of the International Council of Religious Education (ICRE) document, *Christian Education Today,* summarized the discussions of a decade and put forth a rationale for the partnership in large and banal terms: "Families need the Church" [53] and "The Church needs the family." [54] I shall examine each of these propositions in turn.

The families, they said, ". . . need the sustenance and encouragement which can come from a venerable, continuous and powerful institution which shares so fully their purposes and ideals and is dedicated to conserving their basic values." [55] As the extended family in the past had provided a sense of continuity and stability in the lives of its members, so today the church could nurture and protect the nuclear families— now largely isolated from supporting kin and tradition— within its membership.[56] Here was a doctrine of the church that made sense to the religious educators and would also appeal (they hoped) to a family-conscious laity. In protecting and re-enforcing the virtues of family life, Protestantism might once again find its rightful function in society.

"The Church needs the family" because of its power as an agent of social change. Like all educators, whatever their context of faith and work, the liberals proceeded in philosophy and practice according to an underlying theory of social change. The earlier leaders in the religious education movement had been decisively aware of the relation of education and social change. Their successors in the late 1930's and 1940's, beset by changing winds of doctrine, were less articulate or reflective about this matter. Yet both generations looked upon the family as a most powerful matrix of social change. Some, in fact, ventured further and claimed that the family was a primary *source* (as well as matrix) of social change in American society.

In 1938, for instance, Paul H. Vieth of Yale Divinity School and one of the spokesmen for the second generation was bold enough to say: "The family has what is probably the strongest influence of all in shaping not only ideas of right and wrong, but also conduct, ideas and practices of worship, Church affiliation and practice, politics, taste in literature and art, and the development of a philosophy of life." [57] Vieth's estimate, repeated at intervals in the following years, was never seriously criticized. It appeared in slightly modified form in the ICRE's statement, *Christian Education Today:* "The nature and function of the family gives it distinct advantages in Christian education. It has the growing person first and it has him for the largest amount of time during the years of greatest responsiveness and modifiability." [58]

The family, therefore, was the hope of religious education. Those who wrote *Christian Education Today* declared the liberal educator's reliance upon it with forthrightness. "So strategic and strong are the educational influences of the family that the Church's educational purposes as a whole are dependent in large measure upon their Christian quality." [59] If American Protestantism could only harness the family's power, then ". . . the Church could multiply the resources of Christian influences upon her individual members." [60] It was the lure of this distant possibility, more than anything else, that made the partnership seem so important as the next breakthrough in educational strategy.

Both these propositions issued out of wishful thinking and an inept social analysis. Who, besides the convinced churchmen, would be moved to action by the statement that "families need the church"? Or by the inference that the church could serve the family better than other institutions? The latter arose out of a lame effort in apologetics.

Even more fundamentally, it reflects a misunderstanding of

life in the church. The liberal educators had little sense of the Church's one vocation and the many institutional forms for the expression of that single vocation—that is, the congregation gathered for worship and then scattered, living in separate families. The fluid movement between the church's gathered and dispersed life had become a hoped-for relation between two autonomous institutions, each in need of the other.[61] In this respect the rationale represented a secularized map of existence in the church.

It was also an inadequate map of life in American society. In most matters the religious educators were open—almost too open, according to their later critics—to the insights of the social scientists. Yet in this instance, they ignored the corrective of those sociologists who were insisting that the family reflects change as often as it initiates change.[62] No one, for example, pressed Mr. Vieth's assumption far enough to ask the question, What are the sources of the family's understanding of ". . . ideas and practices of worship, Church affiliation and practice, politics," and so on? Their analysis of education and social change was largely a "private" one; it was confined to the private sphere of home and neighborhood. As individuals, of course, they were concerned about what went on in the "public" sphere of politics and economics. But the movement, during its slow decline in the 1930's and 40's, did not have a social analysis that took account of the interaction between the private and public spheres.[63] And so its followers often lapsed into exaggerated claims for the primacy of the family and hence for the promise of the partnership.

The cycle of hope and disappointment, so typical of the history of Protestant educational strategy, was about to start again. Ironically enough, it was the fate of the postliberal educators in the 1940's and 1950's (some of whom had tried so hard to extricate themselves from the liberal tradition) to ride the same roller coaster as had their liberal predecessors during the previous part of the century.

## The New and the Old

"There is a 'conventional wisdom,' to borrow from John Kenneth Galbraith, in education as well as economics, and by the end of World War II, progressivism had come to be that conventional wisdom." [64] Mr. Cremin's judgment would have to be amended if applied to the religious education movement. By 1945 the crest of the movement had long since passed, and the survivors were barely hanging on, embattled and defensive. At midcentury "religious education" seemed stale and lifeless. In the previous decades the religious educators had made an ideology out of assaulting custom and tradition; now they suffered the anomalous indignity of being criticized as conventional by those who appealed to ancient tradition and advocated a "neo-orthodox" theology.

For a while during the fifties there were hints here and there of a new movement in the making. The first and most dramatic sign of a break with the liberal tradition came in the publication of the Faith and Life Curriculum of the Presbyterian Church, U.S.A., issued in 1948 and popularly known as the "New Curriculum." The story of this postliberal venture is worth telling (even in summary form [65]), for it reflects the major trends in recent Protestant thinking about educational strategy.

### The New Curriculum

In many ways it was a new curriculum. The Presbyterians' editor-in-chief, James D. Smart, an Old Testament scholar by training and a pastor well-versed in contemporary and Reformed theology, was not at all inclined to take his travel directions from the old-style religious educators. Together with his associates at the Board of Christian Education, he hammered out a denominational program that was serious and consistent in its theological intent. That fact alone made it something of a novelty in Protestant education.

The "Faith and Life" theology was briskly "neo-Reformed" in orientation. By implication that meant a repudiation of the liberal inheritance, an exodus from the land of religious education. And what were the "fleshpots of Egypt" to be left behind? In Smart's later *apologia* there was a stirring indictment of this particular "Egypt": its pervasive moralism, a tendency to equate Christian and moral education, and a lamentable indifference to the task of thinking theologically about education.[66]

Yet the architects of the "New Curriculum" also persisted in thinking and acting like their liberal forefathers. One of the hidden continuities with the past was indicated in the formal title of the curriculum: "Christian Faith: A Program for Church and Home." They built the family-church school alliance into their program—without, however, subjecting this notion to the same kind of theological criticism that they lavished in such an exciting way upon many of the other ideas of the religious educators.

For many Protestants the partnership theme exemplified the newness of the new curriculum. Shortly after its publication, other denominational agencies were under renewed pressure to revamp their offerings and so keep pace with the Presbyterians. Even those educators who were admittedly cool to the theological orientation of the "Faith and Life" curriculum embraced this innovation. By the early 1950's any number of Protestant editors were busily at work devising their own version of the family-church school alliance.[67]

Though others were imitating their example, the Presbyterian staff was dismayed by the wry discovery that the partnership was not working—at least not to their satisfaction. Reports from the "field" were discouraging; apparently parents had not understood the terms of the alliance. William B. Kennedy recounts their efforts to understand these disappointing results:

[Ralph N.] Mould had prophesied that the home-church tie would perhaps turn out to be the most important single contribution of the new curriculum. It was certainly proving to be the toughest feature to master. And it was to continue to be the most troublesome. Five years later [Norman] Langford reviewed the policy. . . . He admitted frankly that in practice they had weakened "the original purpose of intense home collaboration" because of the unenthusiastic response in family participation. Actually, he stated, "throughout the history of the curriculum primary reliance has been placed on the Church school and on other programs centering in the Church institution." As reasons for the frustration in the parent program Langford listed emphasis upon the Church school, lack of incentive for the parent to study theological material, traditional assumptions of "family religion" in terms of a "family piety that appeals to the convinced," and lack of attention devoted to parental problems and understanding of children and youth.[68]

In other sectors of American Protestantism the story was much the same. None of the main-line denominations had any substantial success in working along the family-church school axis. By 1960 one could glimpse modest gains here and there, probably more of a concern with the churches' ministry to families, but no breakthrough to a new first commitment in educational strategy.

And by now (1964) there is relatively little attention being given to this option; the conversation among church educators has moved on to new possibilities. To illustrate: Wesner Fallaw, one of the early proponents of the partnership between church school and home, has recently come forth with a fresh version of an old idea—a program of church education in the after-school hours of children and youth. In developing his plea for this kind of *Church Education for Tomorrow,* he briefly reviewed the history of Protestant strategy in the nineteenth century. "That is past history," he said, "but a history that turned to the Sunday schools ought now to be made to take a new tack." [69] Yet that history has an energy and thrust all its own—as is evident in the most recent Protestant attempt to go on a "new tack." Nowadays it is tempting to dismiss the experience of the 1950's as a programmatic misfire—which, indeed, it was—and then concentrate upon other alternatives. Protestants, however, might well take another look at this episode, lest its significance be covered over by the nervous gesture of adopting a new scheme.

## A History of Failure

It is, in retrospect, an integral part of a history of reform. Since the turn of the century a few educators in each generation have sought to refurbish the dual system. In the early decades the proponents of the weekday program (Athearn and his contemporaries) worked for a new balance between public and church education, though without notable success. The 1930's and 1940's constituted something of an interim, a period of attempted recovery and slow death for the movement, but also a time for sporadic exploration of future possibilities.

After World War II the cycle of active reform began anew. The church educators of the postwar years were very much in the tradition of the earlier progressives. With rare exception,[70] they continued to assume the parallel arrangement of public and church school. That too was a part of the conventional wisdom; only it went unnoticed and unchallenged amidst the theological fireworks of the last decade. Instead, the postliberal educators mounted a vigorous attack upon the theological rationale of their predecessors. They were not, however, able to replace it with anything equally compelling for a new generation. Their thoughtful restatements of the biblical teachings about the Church—the Body of Christ, the people of God, the new Israel—were interesting, momentarily intriguing, but finally unconvincing. Thus far the postliberal efforts have lacked a formative power, the capacity to shatter old meanings and create new ones. Except for scattered successes in the local outposts of the "renewal" movement, the theologically self-conscious educators of recent years have not been able to dent the Protestant consciousness. Consequently, the appeals for the partnership were largely ignored or misunderstood.

The circle soon came full sweep. In the experience of the Presbyterian editors, for example, one can readily discern some continuities from an earlier time: the alternation between enthusiasm and discouragement, the recurring return to a "primary reliance" (Langford's phrase) upon the Sunday school, and thus a failure to go much beyond the nineteenth-century expression of the dual system. In sum, several generations of church educators, living in varying theological climates, had tried and failed in their respective attempts to alter the status quo.

What of the future? The "history that turned to the Sunday schools" will not be easily deflected onto a "new tack." Indeed, such a redirection may not come at all. If it does, it will be the work of those who understand the power of this history and are therefore willing to acknowledge the present-ness of the past in the "typical Protestant parallelism."

# 3 A NEW OCCASION

Not long before his death, H. Richard Niebuhr described the characteristic Protestant openness to the future in the following way:

> More light is always to break forth from the Scriptures; new occasions will teach new duties. The pragmatism, the experimentalism, the changefulness of order in Protestantism, perhaps particularly in America, may be due in considerable part to the sense of orientation in a dynamic, divinely governed world.[1]

In the coming years this "sense of orientation" will be subject once again to a crucial test, for a new occasion in American education is in the making. It is faintly visible in such innovations as the "new mathematics" and the "new physics." These curricular reforms foretell a larger attempt to make the schools responsive to the accelerating demands of a technological society that is beset by strife over educational policies. The issues are multiple—it is not only a matter of what and how we teach but also where and under what auspices. Is there any way, for instance, to overcome the dangerous color line between central city and suburban school systems? What is the future of the neighborhood schools? Should federal aid go to both parochial and public schools? Does the blending of public and private resources make for good public policy?

These are issues of fateful consequence. In struggling with

51

them, the American people will be moving into a formative period, one as productive of changes and future patterns of action as the time between 1830 and 1860. Doubtless this new occasion will teach new duties. And if American Protestants are to respond appropriately, they will need a full measure of the "pragmatism, the experimentalism" of which Niebuhr spoke—not just an expedient interest in faddish programs, but a deeper restlessness with the inherited order of thought.

The first of our "new duties," I believe, is to become aware of the widening breach between traditional convictions and the demands of the future that is now breaking in upon us. A good place to begin that inquiry is with a critical analysis of some of the attitudes accompanying the "typical Protestant parallelism."

## A Vanishing Point of Contact

In 1962 the United States Supreme Court announced its judgment [2] about the legal propriety of a short, bland "nondenominational" prayer composed by the New York Board of Regents and recited in a Long Island public school. This single act marked the beginning of one of those seasons of confusion, turbulence, and ill-tempered rhetoric that occasionally settles in upon the American public. One year after the "Regents' prayer" case, the Court ruled that a devotional reading of the Bible and the use of the Lord's Prayer in the public school classroom were likewise unconstitutional.[3] The more temperate tone of the 1963 decision did little to mollify the Court's opponents. In the spring of 1964, for example, Congress was besieged by the supporters of the so-called "Becker Amendment," a measure that would abridge the First Amendment to allow religious ceremonies in the schools. This dubious proposal elicited an astonishing response from the public. In the ironic judgment of one observer: "Although the newspapers have devoted more space to the long civil rights debate in the

Senate, the volume of Congressional mail might lead one to believe that the school prayer issue is by far the most important matter being discussed on Capitol Hill this spring." [4] And so the force of the controversy continues, diminishing slightly perhaps, but still felt in many quarters.

But no matter how dismal this season happens to be, it still constitutes an important "sign of the times" for American Protestantism; it should provoke a re-examination of the parallelism.

The decisions—when considered apart from the attendant reaction—are not particularly significant. The Court was completing a process begun years ago in many communities and states [5] : the gradual elimination of the practices of the Protestant-dominated common school of the last century. The devotional reading of the Bible and classroom prayers are among the last remnants to be stripped away.

One need not approve the high Court's decision in all particulars in order to see their larger historical meaning for Protestantism. Even though these rulings are not graced by any consistent judicial logic, they are nevertheless consistently helpful to Protestants at one point: they remind us that we cannot go home again, that is, back to the nineteenth century. Any appeal to past prerogatives is now impossible, except for those afflicted with a Currier and Ives nostalgia for agrarian America. Public schools can no longer embody just the Protestant ethos if they are to be genuinely *public* institutions. In a society such as ours, it is clearly unrealistic and irresponsible to depend upon the public school as a silent partner in the task of Christian education. We can rightfully claim only one thing of these schools: they must offer a truly *public* education. The Protestant can expect a quality of education that is critically responsive to the full reality of public experience, past and present. To hope for anything more, to hark back to the days when Protestantism and the public schools were covert allies, is—in effect—to lapse into reactionary reveries about a time that is no more.

## Making Good Citizens

This much is surely obvious. But what is equally apparent
—and even more significant—is the continuing uneasiness of
the American people about these rulings. This reaction in-
cludes many Protestants and "others" too, all united in suspicion and bewilderment about the intent of the Court. In
some instances resistance amounts to a refusal to abandon any
possible opportunity for religious instruction in the Judeo-
Christian tradition. For the majority, however, it means something different. It signifies a tremor in the American psyche
at the thought of the public schools' departure from the work
of moral education.

The importance of moral training was one of the characteristic appeals of the lawyers who defended the legitimacy of
these practices. Bible reading and classroom prayers, they
said, constitute important occasions for the development of
good character. The Supreme Court did not find their argument very impressive (nor, for that matter, did the intellectuals and theologians). But I suspect that a different verdict
would have been rendered if the same case had been taken to
the American people. Consider, for instance, the spontaneous
response of Harry S. Truman. Out for his morning walk in
New York City, the former President told reporters that his
first-grade teacher had opened the school with prayer. "It
never hurt anybody," he said. "It *made good citizens out of
them.*" [6] On this score, Mr. Truman spoke for many of his
fellow countrymen. These acts of piety symbolize the way in
which the public school engages in the making of "good citizens." Thus the Court's action appeared—in the judgment of
countless Americans—to hinder the school from assuming one
of its proper responsibilities.

Actually, moral education in the public schools is jeopard-
ized by other troubles of far greater import. As a cause, it has
attracted more than its fair share of knaves (running the
gamut from politicians who delight in safe, "moral" issues, to
those in search of one solution for all manner of social ills).

Yet even its most distinguished advocates are hard-pressed to be specific about its meaning and procedure in present-day American society. So much of what is currently proposed in the name of moral education reflects a hidden yearning to recapture the simplicities of an earlier day.

This "back to God . . . morality . . . spiritual values . . . McGuffey's readers" orientation is understandable, if not very helpful. In the nineteenth century Horace Mann could draw upon the consensus of his time to provide the *substance* of the moral training for public school children. Since then, of course, there have been drastic changes in the American sense of morality. Peter Schrag has described this development with pungent accuracy:

> The moral certitudes of traditional America were all part of the school system; when they were finally challenged, they were challenged not by pluralism in religion, by atheistic judges, or by a new surge of constitutional separatism, but by an empirical diet they were never meant to withstand: Heisenberg and Einstein, Lenin and Castro, Hitler and Mao, Ford and Carnegie. . . .
>
> So far, however, America has found no official substitute for the old certitudes. During the past fifty years its official policies have shifted all the way from moralistic progressivism, motivated by a desire to restore the blessings associated with an earlier day, to a pragmatic but optimistic liberalism, and then to a complacent utilitarianism, rooted in an affirmation that this is a Complicated World.[7]

With the unraveling of the ". . . moral certitudes of traditional America" has come an increasing abstraction, a blurry indefiniteness in the formulations of programs of moral education. A case in point is the document, *Moral and Spiritual Values in the Public Schools,* issued by the Educational Policies Commission of the National Education Association in 1951. In this statement a representative group of educators and laymen sought to allay the fears of those who were complaining about the "godlessness" of the public schools. The fruit of their labor was an illustration of committee-report morality: a composite list of ten American values (moral responsibility, brotherhood, devotion to truth, and others),[8] replete with instructions about the application of these values in school life. The values were described in a manner general enough to please the diffuse sentiments of the American people, but not so specific as to suggest a particular action or offensive conflict. So it turned out, as one observer has noted, that ". . . the most extensive program to promote 'moral and spiritual values' as yet undertaken in an American school system, that of Louisville, Kentucky, seems to have been remarkably successful in avoiding the issue of desegregation. The ethics of booing at basketball games appears to have bulked far larger as a problem than that of race relations. . . ."[9]

The genteel idealism of the NEA pronouncement was successful in evoking memories of past certitude (and therein lies the probable source of its appeal in the 1950's); but it did not illumine the present predicaments of moral education. Indeed, that may be an impossible demand to make of the writers of any such consensual document. For, as Neil J. McCluskey, S.J., has said, ". . . the American people have been caught in an unresolved ambiguity. They have charged the common school with the responsibility for character education, but they do not have a common view as to what this entails."[10] That ambiguity is apt to remain unresolved into the future. The bitter aftermath of the Court's ruling is a foretaste of a protracted period of debate and reappraisal that lies before us. In the past months some Americans have voiced (though often in an inchoate and self-defeating manner) their convictions about the public schools' responsibility in moral education; now in the years ahead this nation will come to recognize, even more than at present, the extent of its disagreement over the ways of achieving this end.

This turn of events raises a host of questions for main-line Protestantism. If the Supreme Court decisions and the ensuing response symbolize the final stage in the cultural disestablishment of the churches, so it should also mark the beginning of a search for a new interpretation of the relation between public and church education. What is the character of this relationship in present-day America? Where now is the point of convergence in their respective purposes? It may still reside—as some will doubtless say—in the making of moral men. Yet the meaning of that traditional claim is not self-evident any longer. The nineteenth-century image of the tie between public and Sunday school—a *legal separation* at the level of auspices; a *marriage* at the level of social function—can be maintained today only at the cost of ignoring our increasing difficulties in defining the ways of moral education. That is too high a price to pay; it involves the danger of embracing an empty expectation, a fetching bit of ideology that recalls bygone glories and conveniently obscures the realities of the present.

But to reject that image is not to be done with the parallelism. Its legacy still lingers elsewhere.

### A Pattern of Default

The impress of the past is strikingly evident in the approach of main-stream Protestantism to public education. By way of illustration, I would point to some of the denominational and interdenominational pronouncements in this area. These documents are often informed by a common pattern of thinking: [11] a selective inattention to the larger range of educational policy issues, and a concentration upon certain church-state issues in education. Let us examine each of these emphases in turn.

The first tendency might be ascribed to a needed modesty, an unwillingness to venture beyond one's competence into the technical matters of curriculum, school finances, and the like. I believe, however, that there is another explanation that is even more to the point. One source of this selective inattention is a deeply held (and therefore largely unconscious) belief in the inherent and inevitable harmony of public education and the Protestant cause. Because of a continuing confidence in this institution, American Protestantism has not been constrained to think about national educational policy as a whole. For the most part, the spokesmen for the denominations and the councils have confined themselves to the role of the protector of public education. Our task, they seemed to be saying, is to fend off its opponents—those detractors who complain about its alleged "godlessness," or those rival ecclesiastical groups who want to raid its treasury. Such a defense has often been necessary. But no less necessary, I would submit, is the development of a sustained critique of the public school and its policies.

The omission of this critique is all the more startling when one reflects upon the emergence of a Protestant social ethic over the last six decades. In the course of these years Protestant churchmen have developed a critical perspective upon almost all the sectors of American life. The most conspicuous exception is public education. For example, in reviewing the literature of the social gospel, one is hard-pressed to discover any full appraisal of this institution and its prevailing policies. Often the schools were considered "Christianized" and therefore outside the perimeter of concern. In a statement representative of his time and contemporaries, Walter Rauschenbusch declared:

> Thus our educational system has passed through a regenerating process. As with the family and the Church, the line of progress ran from tyranny to freedom, from aristocratic privilege to democracy of opportunity, from self-seeking to the enthusiasm of service. . . . A constitutional change has taken place which may be justly called a Christianizing of the educational organization.[12]

Although the following generation of Protestant ethicists were loath to distinguish so sharply between the Christian and non-Christian institutions, they were not any more inclined to include the public school in their critical evaluation of American life.[13] Hence, the tendency toward selective inattention.

## The Church-State Focus

By and large the Protestant reflection about educational policy has centered upon the maintenance of some church-state positions—"no public aid for parochial schools" and the like. Such a preoccupation is, of course, partly due to ecclesiastical self-interest. That is particularly true in the matter of governmental funds for Roman Catholic parochial schools. And it will continue to be so, despite the euphoria encouraged by the ecumenical spirit of recent years. For Protestants as well as Catholics, the debate over this issue is more than a gentlemen's disagreement over constitutional law; it is also a race for institutional advantage and competitive position. The Protestant, to be sure, can quickly see how the Catholic Church might benefit from governmental aid. What he cannot admit so candidly is his fear that any such move would upset the status quo and leave Protestant church education even further behind. Meanwhile, in spite of Mrs. Ryan's spirited declaration that the "siege" is over, the "siege mentality" appears to be as strong as ever among some Catholics.

Yet neither side's arguments can be reduced to the single element of self-interest. Both make significant claims for their interpretation of the common good.

Look, for the moment, at the usual Protestant objection to direct governmental subsidy of a parochial school. It is prompted by a genuine abhorrence of what subsidized pluralism might do to American education. John C. Bennett, surely one of the most irenic interpreters of Protestant-Catholic differences, makes this point vividly:

> I am told by those who have studied the matter most closely that we could not expect to have fewer than five or six systems of parochial schools competing for the resources of the community in the large or middle-sized cities. This would be divisive; it would be expensive; and it would also mean that every system would be educationally weak. It would mean a scattering of our available personnel and of our available funds.[14]

Here Mr. Bennett voices a concern that is shared by many Americans, including a growing number of Roman Catholics.

Yet the Protestant conception of the common good goes deeper. It is rooted in the nineteenth-century conviction, whose historical staying power I have noted throughout this essay: the public school is America's unique solution to a pressing issue—unity in diversity. Thus many people would agree with James B. Conant's now famous charge:

> The greater the proportion of our youth who fail to attend our public schools and who receive their education elsewhere, the greater the threat to our democratic unity. To use taxpayers' money to assist private schools is to suggest that American society use its own hands to destroy itself.[15]

But is this argument as compelling as once was the case? I think not. It is subject to at least three criticisms.

• The Conant-type argument may be a handy weapon for Protestants to use in the fierce ideological warfare over public funds for parochial schools. In one respect, however, it involves a doubtful assertion. One can question Mr. Conant's claim for the role of the public school in maintaining "our democratic unity." In this estimate he presumed the vitality of the common school tradition, namely, that the public school continues to be the major institution where persons of diverse classes and races come to know and respect one another. That has been the function of *some* schools in the past. It may still be true of the secondary school in towns or small cities. Yet in what sense can it be descriptive of the contemporary public school in the metropolis? The *de facto* segregated neighborhood school, whether in the suburbs or central city, is not really a common school. (An urban youngster's service in the Armed Forces is probably the closest present-day approximation to an older "common school experience"; there, for the first time, he encounters in a more personal way the diversity of the American people.)

• A second objection was advanced a few years ago by Will

Herberg: "Americanization," he said, "is no longer a problem. Aside from a few immigrants who still come into this country, Americans today are born, not made." [16] Thus he disputed those who presume that the public school is essentially an "engine of Americanization." [17]

> Today the older emphasis on cultural unity and the older fear of divisiveness are not merely out of place; they can well become an oppressive mark in the compulsive conformity that is increasingly the mark of our other-directed culture. Today the emphasis should not be upon unity, except of course the political unity of the nation, but on diversity. And in the effort to safeguard and cultivate diversity, the religious school has a significant role to play. . . .[18]

Since this analysis is often employed by the defenders of the parochial schools, it is sometimes ignored or prematurely dismissed by Protestants. I believe it deserves a better hearing.

The interpretation is, of course, vulnerable to criticism. For instance, the public schools probably promote more diversity than Mr. Herberg managed to see. First, there is some religious variation from one school system to another. The variation is not so much in what is explicitly taught in the classroom as in the ethos sustaining the school. In small-town America the Protestant spirit still affects the life of many a public school. That influence is noticeable in the selection of teachers and in assembly programs, for instance. (A Southern Baptist once said—more by way of complaint than a boast—that the rural public schools in portions of the South constitute, in effect, the Southern Baptist parochial school system.) Compare these schools, then, with an urban school in a Northeastern metropolis; the difference in ethos is considerable.

There is, second, a considerable variation among public schools because of social stratification. The "natural" grouping of pupils in the neighborhood schools often means segregation according to socio-economic and racial divisions. Here variety is apparent in both the content of instruction and the ethos of the school. Mr. Conant, in his work, *Slums and*

*Suburbs,* has already called attention to the distance between the "slum" school and the one in the suburb.[19] Indeed, there may be as many functional differences between these two types of public schools as there are between the parochial and public schools as a whole.

Even so, Mr. Herberg still has a case—particularly if it is developed in the following manner. The factor of religious variation, he could say, is largely residual; therefore, it will tend to diminish in the coming years. The gap between the "slum" and suburban school represents an obvious social inequity—not true diversity—and should be closed as much as possible. Furthermore, Protestants might well reconsider their pride in the public school as "a major cohesive force in our pluralistic society." [20] In stressing the imperative of cultural unity, Protestant spokesmen unwittingly adhere to a theory of public education that was formulated well before the advent of radio, television, and other means of national communication. Consequently, they are slow to recognize the contours of the present situation in which the schools—either in the parochial or public systems—are intimately interlinked with other powerful unifying agents. In this setting the central problem is not cultural unity but, instead, the *quality* of our national culture. Paul Goodman has set forth just that thesis in angry and harsh terms:

> It is in the schools and from the mass media, rather than at home or from their friends, that the mass of our citizens in all classes learn that life is inevitably routine, depersonalized, venally graded; that it is best to toe the mark and shut up; that there is no place for spontaneity, open sexuality, free spirit. Trained in the schools, they go on to the same quality of jobs, culture, politics. This *is* education, mis-education, socializing to the national norms, and regimenting to the national "needs." [21]

I do not care to defend all that Mr. Goodman says or implies, but it is a judgment worth pondering—one that should be answered and corrected (if possible) in any future Protestant interpretation of public education.

• Yet the center of the problem for the American educator
has moved somewhat beyond the point where Will Herberg
located it. It is not so much "the older emphasis on cultural
unity" or Mr. Herberg's version of diversity as it is *competence*. By competence, I mean the capacity for continuous
productive learning, the ability to stay responsive and rational
amidst the flux of change in a technological society. But, the
reader might object, was not this also the task of the educator
a century ago? Yes—but not to the same intensive degree
that is true nowadays. Solon T. Kimball and James E. Mc-
Clellan, Jr., in their provocative analysis of the nineteenth-
century school, write:

> It is clear that for anyone who was going to remain stationary
> in his agrarian community, all that he would need to know, in
> terms of knowledge, skills, and attitudes, he could learn *without*
> schooling. What he could not learn without formal instruction
> was how to move and change. And as the conditions of life
> changed around him, not to move and change was to fall behind.
> Hence, the fact of *being* schooled became of great importance,
> while the content of that schooling remained a secondary mat-
> ter.[22]

Now, plainly enough, the "content of . . . schooling" is no
longer a "secondary matter." Since the launching of the Soviet
satellite, Sputnik, the American people in general—and the
educators, in particular—have been exposed to an avalanche
of advice about the appropriate intellectual fare for our school
population. The reasons for this development are quite diverse: the "let's-bury-the-Russians" motivation for educational
reform; a longstanding dismay within the scientific communities over the poor preparation of their recruits; and, perhaps
less obviously, but more fundamentally, the pressures of a
technological economy for new levels of training and skill.
The recentness of these accelerating demands becomes most
visible when we examine the plight of the school in the urban
ghettos (where, indeed, most of the other contradictions in
American life are evident). So Christopher Jencks has stated:

The slum school is now being asked to do in one generation what it formerly did in three, and it can't do it. Instead of making the first generation off the farm into literate but unskilled factory workers, making their children into craftsmen, office employees, and small businessmen, and their grandchildren into professional and managerial experts, the slum school must complete the whole cycle at once.[23]

These changes have brought about a new direction in the ongoing conversation about education. Today it swirls around such questions as—What form of curriculum and manner of instruction will most likely develop the continuously productive learner? [24] How can formal education provide that "take-off" point so necessary if one is to have the power of participation in the future? [25]

What is under dispute, in sum, is the source of this competence and the ends it should serve. There is no need, at least in this monograph, to describe the positions of the various participants in this debate.[26] For our purposes here, the most striking fact about this discussion is its location. It has been going on steadily within the university, occasionally among school personnel, but seldom, if ever, in the churches and the seminaries.

I hope that Protestant scholars will soon join this conversation, for it involves issues of consummate public importance. But the ability to do so requires a willingness to venture beyond a preoccupation with the usual church-state problems, a newfound attentiveness to the larger range of educational policy—in short, a freedom from the pattern of default described in these pages.

## A Marginal Enterprise

In studying a prestigious suburban settlement, a team of social scientists noted the declining influence of church education upon the decisions and loyalties of middle-class parents. For most of the inhabitants of "Crestwood Heights," the public school was the central, pivotal institution; their involvement in its life was a major "social source" of understanding of education, whether in school, church, or elsewhere. The authors of *Crestwood Heights* portrayed the newness of this power alignment by way of the following diagram: [27]

*Patterns of Dominance* (circa 1850 [left] and 1950 [right]

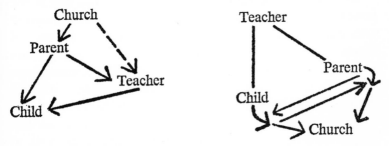

This diagram, if amended,[28] serves as a crude symbol of a historical trend—the increasing marginality of Protestant church education in the total sweep of American education.

Consider, in a backward glance, the changes over the past one hundred years in Protestantism's relative power as a sponsor of formal education. In the middle decades of the nineteenth century the Sunday school compared more favorably with the nascent public school of that time than is presently the case. Protestants were then very much in the business of higher education; nowadays there is a steadily declining percentage of church-related institutions among the total number of colleges and universities.

The most startling contrast lies in the field of adult education. Even as late as the 1920's the Protestant churches were among the pioneers in developing that unexplored territory. But within the last two decades the leadership in formal adult education has clearly passed to such new powers as the Armed Forces and the large corporations. This shift foretells a larger movement that will be more evident in the coming years. One of the distinctive marks of existence in a technological economy is the necessity of continuing formal education throughout a person's productive life. In the days ahead an expanding public-private effort—including a complex of state-sponsored programs, community "adult colleges" sparked by local initiative and industry-backed ventures in continuing education—will help to make continuing education a reality for an increasing number of Americans.

What will be the future place of the churches amidst the growing array of educational agencies? One can reasonably anticipate that the churches' efforts in formal education will become even more marginal when compared with the activities of public and other nonpublic institutions. This prediction applies alike to Roman Catholicism and Protestantism. Without extensive federal support, the Catholic school system can at best accommodate a diminishing portion of the rising population of Catholic youth. So Philip Scharper has said:

> . . . The goal of "every Catholic child in a Catholic school" was unrealistic when uttered by the Third Plenary Council of Baltimore in 1884—and it will be less, not more, realistic in 1984.

> . . . By 1985 approximately 75% of the Catholics in the 18-24 bracket may be in non-Catholic colleges and universities, while at least one projection suggests that 80-90% of high school-age Catholics will not be in Catholic schools. American Catholics, then, are coming to accept public education for the same reasons which ultimately forced Margaret Fuller to accept the universe.[29]

Protestants—in the main—embraced that particular "universe" long ago. In the years ahead, therefore, they may be somewhat insulated from the pain and turmoil of the Catholic experience. The internal debate among Catholics over educational strategy is now in full swing; and the acrimonious reception of Mary Perkins Ryan's essay *Are Parochial Schools the Answer?* indicates how heated it might become.

Whatever the outcome of this struggle, American Catholicism will not, contrary to the hopes of some Protestants, "finally come around" to the solution of the Sunday school and family nurture. There will continue to be significant differences. I doubt that Catholic education will ever become as marginal in the whole enterprise of American education as its Protestant counterpart.

For one reason, the Catholics will be quicker to participate in a characteristic aspect of the new occasion in American education: the explicit and purposeful intermeshing of private and public efforts in schooling. The practice of public-private co-operation, now so evident in other spheres of activity in our society, is presently visible at the level of the graduate school. By degrees it will become increasingly evident at the lower rungs of the educational ladder. That change could come about in one of several ways—in shared-time programs or else in governmental aid for parochial schools. If federal aid goes to the public schools alone, there will be increasing pressure for the development of shared-time arrangements across the country. If, on the other hand, government funds are also granted to parochial schools, then Protestants will have to consider seriously (probably for the first time since the nineteenth century) the feasibility of church-sponsored day schools. In either event, there will be a complementary use of private and public resources (finances or personnel) in a common educational undertaking. And, in either event, the Catholic Church is ready to move in a way that is not true of main-stream Protestantism.

*Shared Time*

That difference is most clearly reflected in the probable Catholic and Protestant responses to shared time.[30] Once again, after an interval of nearly forty years, there is considerable talk about this option in educational strategy. In the 1950's a few Protestants made tentative proposals in this direction.[31] Yet it was a proposal of Harry L. Stearns, formerly the superintendent of schools in Englewood, New Jersey, that finally caught the public's attention. He said:

Simply stated the idea of shared time involves the division of the time of school children between public schools and church schools: certain subjects would be taught in the public schools to all children; other subjects—specifically those of religious content —would be taught to all or part of the same children in church schools of the parents' choice. For example, a Protestant child may study a considerable number of the traditional subjects in the public high school and also attend, during some portion of his school time, a church school where he receives fuller-than-at-present instruction in religious education.[32]

Mr. Stearns went on to enumerate the many difficulties inherent in this scheme. It would require a new flexibility on the part of the public school administrator as he meets the problems of scheduling, academic credits, and the probable need for new school buildings. Shared time would also exact something new from the churches. "Without united church support," he warned, "there is little chance of moving it forward." [33]

He did not, however, consider the most important question about the responses of the churches to shared time. Mr. Stearns assumed that "the prospect of gaining a larger share of the child's time for a chuch-conducted program should be welcome to many church people." [34] But is that true? Here one would have to distinguish rather sharply between the likely Catholic and Protestant reactions.

The story of the varying fortunes of the released-time program provides a possible clue as to future Catholic participation in shared time. The comparison is an apt one, for the development of released time was considerably influenced by the ideas of those who were proposing plans for shared time in the early decades of this century.[35] Leo Pfeffer has summarized the Roman Catholic reaction in this way:

The released-time program had been a Protestant experiment originating before World War I. For some thirty years American Catholicism was indifferent to it. Few bishops bothered with it, preferring to concentrate the educational efforts of their dioceses on the parochial schools. With the McCollum decision the situation changed radically. The Catholic Church became the most ardent advocate of the released-time plan. More and more Catholic school systems began to participate in it. What was originally a pan-Protestant device quickly became a predominantly Catholic instrument, particularly in large urban areas. . . . It is not too much to say that the released-time plan depends for its existence on Catholic support and that if the Catholic Church returned to its previous position of indifference and noncooperation, the program would soon collapse.[36]

I would guess that the same pattern of events might hold fast in the future if shared time becomes a lively possibility.

What about the Protestant response? Would Protestants in the main-line denominations welcome ". . . the prospect of gaining a larger share of the child's time for a church-conducted program?" In all likelihood, shared time would involve the further prospect of supporting an enlarged school budget, and at the same time providing the requisite funds for the development of adequate building space and a professionally trained staff for a church program. Shared time would test the morale of the Protestant parent in a way only faintly envisioned in the original proposals for the family-Sunday school partnership. It could also require of him an acceptance of a longer school day, a willingness to forego his children's participation in some of the extracurricular activities now available, and above all a sustaining conviction about the inalienable and unique importance of church education. Would such a parental response be forthcoming?

For the time being, at least, these questions are difficult to answer in any authoritative way. Yet it is significant to note the implied verdict given by many of the current advocates of shared time. Earlier in the century Walter S. Athearn and his peers looked upon this option as a solution to a distinctly Protestant quandary, namely, how to expand the institutional bases for church education. Now it has become—at least in many Protestant circles—the favorite prescription for all the ills afflicting Catholic parochial schools. This embrace of shared time reflects both a concern for some resolution of the current impasse over federal aid to education, and also an assumption (widely held but as yet untested by debate) that American Protestantism need not extend itself in this direction.[37]

## Protestants and Parochial Schools

The melding of public and private resources in education might also come by way of governmental subsidy for parochial schools. George R. LaNoue, a close observer of Congressional struggles over aid to education, has predicted that a major turning point in the battle is not far off. "It is likely," he has said, "that sometime in this decade a national decision will be reached on the question of public funds for religious schools." [38]

No one can confidently predict what that decision will be. In the past, legislative proposals on federal aid to education have been "politically accident-prone" [39] bills, ensnared in the web of veto politics. One stumbling block is the Catholic veto of any proposal that does not include some benefits for parochial schools. In parallel fashion Protestants have joined with others in developing a counterveto. The National Council of Churches and the denominations as well have gone on record for federal aid to public education but have become increasingly opposed to any possibility of assistance for the parochial schools. Elsewhere, on the same battleground, there is conflict between the state's-righters and the advocates of federal responsibility. The outcome of all these skirmishes is still in doubt.

But let us suppose, for a moment, that the country moved toward governmental aid for church-sponsored day schools. What would the Protestant response be? To be sure, this is an "iffy" question, one unusually subject to the vagaries of history. Even so, it is an important question to raise, since few Protestants have thought beyond the present battle to that future time when this uninvited opportunity might overtake the main-stream denominations.

In all likelihood it would come in the form of an uneasy compromise [40]—no general "across the-board" aid for the schools, but rather, limited assistance in classroom instruction, teacher training, and the provision of textbooks. If that were the case, then the established parochial schools would be given a modest boost, enough perhaps to arrest momentarily their decline, yet not enough to guarantee their expansion. In these circumstances would main-stream Protestantism attempt to spawn new systems of church-sponsored day schools?

Undoubtedly some congregations and perhaps even one or more of the major denominations might try to take advantage of these new resources. But the majority, I suspect, would not move in that direction. The most obvious deterrent would be expense. The limited government subsidies would tend to favor existing systems rather than new ones. Without the momentum and facilities of a working institution, the Protestants would be at the mercy of the upward spiral of educational costs.

The tug of tradition also inhibits any concerted move toward this option. After the experience of the last one hundred years, many churchmen are prone to regard the Protestant-sponsored day school as unnecessary and even faintly heretical. John C. Bennett's observation—"There is nothing un-Protestant about the idea of parochial schools" [41]—would hardly surprise a European Protestant. On this side of the Atlantic (where, indeed, it was meant to be heard) it jogs the memory and forces recognition of the presence of a latent conviction, seldom stated in an explicit way but nevertheless determinative of attitudes and action. This suspicion is sustained and reinforced by another conviction of a similar kind. One of the lingering effects of nineteenth-century revivalism is an anti-intellectual distrust of formal church education. Here I would agree with Dean M. Kelley. In explaining the usual indifference of Protestantism toward the church school, he recently said:

This may be due in part to inertia or entropy, but I think it is also due to an unconscious suspicion on the part of many Protestants that classrooms do not accomplish a great deal for the faith as they conceive it. In the Methodist and Baptist traditions especially, there is less emphasis upon an intellectual deposit of faith to be transmitted to the young, and more upon an experimental encounter with the Holy Spirit through the charismatic preaching of the Word primarily to adults and older adolescents.[42]

Such an orientation encourages a satisfaction with the present order of arrangements.

The financial hardship could be cheerfully borne and older attitudes modified if there were any other compelling reasons for Protestants to embrace church-sponsored day schools. Yet I can see no such motivating forces at work in the life of the major denominations. Recall, if you will, the collapse of the family-church school partnership and other experiments designed to broaden the base of Protestant church education. If main-stream Protestantism failed in these modest efforts, then is it likely to muster the morale necessary for the launching of a system of elementary and secondary schools? The most plausible answer is "No"—except, perhaps, in those situations where the day school provides a "respectable" way of avoiding desegregation in public school systems.[43] In short, the decisions of the past will be reconfirmed; the way of the future leads in the direction of an increasing marginality for Protestant church education.

## Drifting with the Times

These comments represent, of course, one man's attempt to anticipate the future. Indeed, that fact may be the most significant thing about the preceding speculations. In this instance there is little else to report. One cannot draw upon any serious studies of the possible courses of action *if* federal aid to religious schools becomes a reality. (The usual tracts which warn against public funds for parochial schools are of little help in this respect.) Nor can one rely upon the insights

emerging out of a sustained debate on this issue among Protestants. The literature is barren and the conversation lacking.
Unfortunately, that same judgment applies all too often to the
discussion of other options in educational strategy.

The sources of this complacent disregard for the future are
various. To name just two of the contributing causes: for all
the complaints about the Sunday school, there continues to be
a residual confidence in the present patterns of church education; and that trust is, in turn, related to an attitude characteristic of nineteenth-century Protestantism—an optimism
about the effectiveness of marginal efforts in church education. These factors, along with many others, account for the
apparent willingness of Protestantism to drift with the times.

One can hope, however, for a more appropriate response
to the "new occasion" and the duty it teaches. Not apathy, of
course, or anger over our cultural displacement—but rather,
a sense of the possibilities of a new Protestant witness on the
margin of American education.

The peculiar opportunities of marginality—in this one instance, at least—are manifold. Main-stream Protestantism is
not encumbered by the burden of a parochial school system
that devours a disproportionate share of the church's time,
energy, and money. (The cost of the Catholic parochial school
system is more than financial; it is often purchased by forfeit-
ing a full-orbed teaching ministry.[44]) Potentially, American
Protestants enjoy the freedom to perceive areas of educational
neglect, the independence needed for developing experimentally oriented programs that the public schools could
learn from, and the possibility of using the church's resources
in continually changing combinations so as to meet emergent
needs. In these ways the churches could be the critic on the
margin, an institution which seeks to sustain and supplement
the variety and quality of education in America.

But that time is not yet. And it will belong to an indefi-
nitely receding future until American Protestants turn their
critical gaze inward and thus attend to some unfinished business of their own.

# 4 SOME UNFINISHED BUSINESS

> Lord, enlighten thou our enemies . . . ; sharpen their wits, give acuteness to their perceptions and consecutiveness and clearness to their reasoning powers. We are in danger from their folly, not from their wisdom. . . .[1]
>
> —John Stuart Mill

Where are the "enemies" of Protestantism's understanding of education? There is an ominous silence on this topic nowadays. (Here is another impressive bit of evidence of marginality.) Almost twenty-five years ago H. Shelton Smith wrote that ". . . the present situation calls less for construction than for unsparing criticism." [2] His work, *Faith and Nurture,* was a remarkable beginning in that direction. Yet in the succeeding years church educators largely ignored the critical task. Consequently, their "constructive" theories of nurture were blighted by what James D. Smart has properly called ". . . the sterility that seems to afflict the so-called 'new theological era in religious education.' " [3]

It is now time to renew the work of "unsparing criticism." And so, in these concluding comments, I shall suggest several lines of inquiry for prospective critics. The following suggestions point in one direction—the responsibility of Protestantism in sustaining the public ventures in education. My emphasis here represents a deliberate reversal of the order of treatment usually accorded the topics of church and public education. Since the turn of the century, Protestant church educators have tended to begin and end with reform of church education. In offering an alternative point of departure, I do not mean to imply an either/or choice, but instead, a corrective of our "natural" inclinations.

### An Inadequate Lens

How can American Protestantism help in sustaining the public ventures in education?

This question rates a high priority on the agenda of any critic in the future. In the past Protestants have not seriously pressed this question because they believed the answer was already within their grasp. That assumption should be tested in the days ahead.

Earlier, I described the common Protestant preoccupation with church-state problems in education. Our tendency is to make this single interest into a lens for viewing the whole enterprise of public education. At its worst, this procedure amounts to a kind of narcissistic folly. But, even at its best, it provides a poor set of spectacles for looking at educational policy. The resulting perceptions are inadequate and subject to distortion.

• *The importance of the church-state issue becomes vastly exaggerated.* This tendency can be seen in the thinking of both the religionizers—those who hanker after the frayed practices of school piety—and the de-religionizers—who want to make the public schools antiseptically free of all traces of religious language and worship activities.

Both camps need to consider the potentially divisive effects of their efforts upon the politics of education. Recently the editors of *The New Republic* cautioned the de-religionizers:

> We need desperately to multiply our schools, to disperse homogeneous neighborhood groups through the systems, and to draw those who are leaving back into the public schools. Is this the time, then, to ventilate the issue of religion in the sort of abso-

lute terms that are certain to alienate many of those whose support is needed because they possess the means to seek an alternative? [4]

Of course not. The job of strengthening the public school systems will require a broad span of political support.

Lawrence A. Cremin, in discussing the history of progressivism in American education, tells how the progressives made a "supreme political blunder" in the 1930's: ". . . the political coalition of businessmen, trade unionists, farmers, and intellectuals that had supported them in their early efforts was simply permitted to crumble." [5] The needed coalition for the 1960's has not yet come into existence. If and when it does, the matter of Bible reading and classroom prayers will rank low in any realistic ordering of imperatives. Will the religionizers and the de-religionizers accept the relatively low priority of their causes?

• *There is often a concomitant failure to sense the interconnection between church-state issues and other policy goals.* There are abundant illustrations of this tendency.[6] In the confines of this monograph I shall cite just one depressing example: the unwillingness of many Protestant spokesmen to confront realistically the relation between the process of desegregating urban public schools and the matter of federal aid to education.

The public schools in New York City provide an unfortunately apt illustration of the difficulties now plaguing other metropolitan centers in the struggle over desegregation. Because of the flight to suburbia there are not enough white middle-class children to integrate properly the public schools. An extensive network of highways, easy FHA mortgage terms, and the middle-class drive for a plot of grass and "good schools" have all contributed to *de facto* segregation in the central city. The policy of open enrollment—that is, allowing parents of children in a highly segregated school district to send them to a school in a somewhat less segregated neighborhood—has proved to be a minor palliative. Furthermore, there are no effective judicial remedies in sight.[7]

In the coming years, therefore, educational and civic leaders face a political challenge of staggering dimensions—the build-up of support (including that of white parents) for either "educational parks," or some form of a massive interchange of students between the central city and suburban school districts. One step in that direction is the upgrading of the predominantly Negro and Puerto Rican schools. The authors of *Youth in the Ghetto,* a sobering document recently issued by Harlem Youth Opportunities Unlimited, Inc. (HARYOU), hit hard on this point:

> Meaningful desegregation of the public schools in New York City can occur only if all of the schools in the system are raised to the highest standards, and when the quality of education in these schools is uniformly high and does not vary according to income or the social status of the neighborhood.[8]

This intermediate move will require an immediate transfusion of new money into the sorely pressed urban systems. Some of the necessary funds could come from local and state sources; much of it, however, will be the responsibility of the federal government.

And here the trail leads back into the thicket of problems surrounding federal aid to education. Among them, of course, is the church-state issue, which ". . . either in its own right or as a smoke screen for . . . others, has regularly served as the No. 1 obstacle when it came right down to Congressional action." [9] American Protestants have a role (albeit a minor one) in the removal of this obstacle. If we care about "meaningful desegregation" and good education for *all* in the metropolis, then we will begin anew in the search for a resolution of the impasse.[10] To commit ourselves in this fashion does not entail capitulation to every Catholic claim upon public funds for parochial schools. It does mean, however, that we should be far more resourceful in seeking out a compromise formula that is constitutional and contributes to good public policy. Otherwise, all of us are caught in the futility of veto politics. And the public schools—particularly the *de facto* segregated schools in the central city—will be the sure losers.

In this instance, as in many others, there is need for critics who will press American Protestants to sense the interconnections between church-state problems and other issues and so move toward a larger vision of the public ventures in education.

### A Larger Vision

There are many ways of describing what might be seen in such a larger vision. I shall give just two illustrations.

• It is time now to go beyond the conventional Protestant stand on the teaching of religion in the public schools. The present thinking of most Protestants on this matter varies little from the formulation developed in the 1930's, that is, such instruction is permissible if it is "objective." George R. La Noue's statement is representative of other contributions along this line:

> Public school teaching, as is stated in the teacher manuals of any public system, must strive toward a balanced neutral presentation of religious questions. Descriptive or empirical teaching about religion is acceptable, but teaching supported by public funds must avoid normative teaching or teaching for commitment.[11]

No one could quarrel with this judgment if it were simply a plea for integrity in curricula materials and fairness in the presentation of diverse points of view. But, obviously enough, it involves more than that. The sharp emphasis upon an absolute distinction between normative and objective teaching is a dubious contribution to good educational policy.

What if the same argument were applied to other areas of controversy, such as politics, economics, or history? It would make education into a dull process of acquiring marketable skills and neutral information. There are already enough schoolmen who prefer the safe, "public relations" approach to lively issues. Why encourage their timidity in exploring the depths and heights of contemporary life? This flatlander version of education misses the point. The critical problem—I would submit—is not the presence of "normative teaching," but rather, the absence of the freedom of intelligent dissent by both teacher and student. The health and vitality of any school depends upon its ability to deal with controversy without fear of reprisal.

On this score there is reason for pessimism. By and large the American public school is timid and anxious in its approach to controversial matters. "When a specific conflict arises," according to Edgar Z. Friedenberg, "the school almost automatically seeks to *mediate* rather than to clarify. It assesses the power of the conflicting interests, works out a compromise among them, and keeps its name out of the papers." [12] This leveling-out process is particularly evident in the school personnel's treatment of the humanities. Mr. Friedenberg's further comments on this point are most instructive, since the study of religion poses comparable problems—and temptations:

> They [the school personnel] fear that students will find passages too difficult, and assume that it is the artist's job to say no more than can be easily understood. They fear that the American Legion or a Catholic action group will object to the implication of other passages, and they also fear that they themselves will be called censors; so rather than suppress a work, they set up committees to *edit* it and forestall any possible objections.[13]

Such are the exigencies of developing a "balanced, neutral presentation."

In this setting the prospects for a lively teaching about religious convictions and institutions are not favorable. But at least Protestant churchmen should reflect on how their appeal for "objective" instruction might be heard in this context. Hopefully, they will venture even further. I would propose the following test for any Protestant action in this area: do our attitudes and recommendations strengthen the resolve of the school to deal with controversy *wherever it may be found?* The study of religion in the public schools will become competent only when the educator is free and willing to exercise his rightful independence from community pressure. Our first intent, therefore, is to help the school be a school and not the frightened shadow of American society. And our first need, therefore, is for informed critics who can demonstrate the intricate relationships between academic freedom, the development of a true profession among public school educators, and the ability to handle explosive issues in the classroom.

• Now comes the most troublesome question of all. Should the comprehensive concern of the Protestant for the public ventures in education include the Catholic parochial school? Here the burden of the past weighs as heavily upon Protestants as it does upon the Catholics. Despite all the words written and said on the subject, there has been very little honest conversation about it. Dean M. Kelley's report of an exchange between Protestant and Catholic leaders nicely symbolizes the ineffectiveness of the ecumenical dialogue at this point:

> Many Roman Catholics insist that parochial schools—at least insofar as they concern the public—are primarily and essentially *educational* institutions, and that their educational function can be viewed as distinct from their religious function. "This is an educational issue, not a religious issue," insisted one Roman Catholic leader, to which a Protestant spokesman responded, "For us, it is a religious issue, not an educational issue." [14]

Surely both claims are misleading.

For the Protestant it is an educational issue as well as a religious one. The Catholic Church in America has taken on the responsibility for educating a sizable number of the population.[15] Up until now American Protestants have been inclined to view this fact as a threat, an all too visible reminder of Catholic power.

But do Protestants have any responsibility toward these schools and their students? I believe that we have the responsibility to reconsider—seriously and without premature polemic dismissal—the following questions proposed by Rabbi Arthur Gilbert:

> Are we prepared to write off 12 per cent of our children as excluded from our concern? Can America afford such a waste? Is it not possible, therefore, to provide educational services for *all* children without regard to the school they attend; or train all teachers without regard to the uniform they wear; or provide laboratories and workshops, testing facilities as well as health and medical benefits and textbooks and transportation for all children without involving the Government in direct aid to one religion over another? [16]

To this list, I would add some further questions. How can Protestant congregations properly express their interest in the local Catholic schools? By offering to co-operate in the production of curricular materials in Christian education? By working alongside Catholics in the political struggles that inevitably accompany responsible experimentation with shared time? By lending an empty Sunday school building to a crowded parochial school? (Even if the Sunday school does not represent "the most wasted hour of the week." [17] nevertheless, the Sunday school building is probably the most wasted building space in America.)

Daniel Callahan, in speaking for the editors of *The Commonweal* said:

> More than once have we wished that the N.C.W.C. would devote some of its energy to these public school matters; that the diocesan papers, which manage to find considerable space for the "Catholic case," would dramatize the plight of the public school; that the bishops, pastors, and lay organizations would put their minds to work on some of these American educational problems which do not directly concern Catholics.[18]

By the same token, a Protestant might say—"Even though the parochial school and public school are not comparable in their importance to the common good, I wish that the National Council of Churches would devote some of its energy to the questions stated above; that the denominational magazines which manage to find considerable space for the case against the Catholic school, would dramatize the plight of these schools; that pastors and laymen would put their minds to work on some of these American educational problems which do not directly concern Protestants." [19]

\* \* \*

These are only a few of the possible lines for any future critic. But when considered together, these suggestions do indicate something of the enormity and excitement of the task now facing American Protestantism. That task, as I interpret it, is to acknowledge the presentness of the past as it is manifest in the "typical Protestant parallelism," to gain our freedom from its legacy in and through renewed historical self-understanding, and then to work toward a new understanding of the relation of public and church education.

# NOTES

## PREFACE

1. Mary Perkins Ryan, *Are Parochial Schools the Answer?: Catholic Education in the Light of the Council* (New York: Holt, Rinehart & Winston, Inc., 1964).
2. *Ibid.*, p. 49.
3. Neil G. McCluskey, S. J., *Catholic Education in America: A Documentary History* (New York: Bureau of Publications, Teachers College, Columbia University, 1964), p. 37.
4. James Hastings Nichols, "Religion and Education in a Free Society" in *Religion in America,* John Cogley, ed. (New York: Meridian Press, Inc., 1958), p. 152.
5. Gordon Harland, "The American Protestant and the Political Task" (an unpublished paper done for the Institute for Religious and Social Studies, 1961), p. 16.
6. One prefatory note is in order. By the phrase "educational strategy" I refer to the Church's selection of certain institutional forms as the means of expressing its educational ministry and the consequent allocation of the Church's human resources of time, energy, and money.

## CHAPTER 1.

1. Louis Wirth, "Preface" in Karl Mannheim, *Ideology and Utopia,* Louis Wirth and Edward Shils, trs. (New York: Harcourt, Brace & World, Inc., 1936), p. xxiv.
2. James Hastings Nichols, "Religion and Education in a Free Society" in *Religion in America,* John Cogley, ed. (New York: Meridian Press, Inc., 1958), p. 148.
3. For a survey of the considerable variety of schools during the colonial period, see Ellwood P. Cubberley, *Public Education in the United States* (Boston: Houghton Mifflin Co., 1934), pp. 26-51.

It is worth noting that a present-day Roman Catholic observer accepts this arrangement as close to the "Catholic educational ideal." See Theodore Maynard, *The Story of American Catholicism* (New York: The Macmillan Company, 1941), p. 458.

The triangle as norm was seldom emphasized—except when it was under attack. For instance, in the struggle over religion in the Massachusetts schools, Horace Mann attributed to his "orthodox" antagonists a covert desire to re-establish the old alignment of church, home, and school. See Raymond Culver, *Horace Mann and the Massachusetts Public Schools* (New Haven: Yale University Press, 1929), pp. 200 f.

5. This movement was actually a continuation of the educational practices from the colonial period—see Conrad H. Moehlman, *School and Church: The American Way* (New York: Harper & Row, Inc., 1944), pp. 66-67. The debate over church-sponsored day schools within some denominations became increasingly important in the middle decades. The best summary of this development is to be found in Lewis J. Sherrill, *Lift Up Your Eyes* (Richmond, Va.: John Knox Press, 1949), pp. 29 f. For a fuller account see Lewis J. Sherrill, *Presbyterian Parochial Schools: 1846-1870* (New Haven: Yale University Press, 1932), pp. 12-13, *et passim.*

Peter H. and Alice S. Rossi have pointed to a significant source of the continuing interest in parochial schools among both Catholics and Protestants: it was the German immigrants (of either Roman Catholic or Lutheran persuasion) who sparked the drive toward parochial schools in their respective communions. Thus today the Lutheran Church—Missouri Synod—has the largest number of church-sponsored day schools of any American Protestant denomination. (For further reference see Peter H. and Alice S. Rossi, "Some Effects of Parochial School Education in America," *Daedalus: Journal of the American Academy of Arts and Sciences,* LXXXX (1961), 300-328.

Fr. Joseph N. Moody adds corroborating evidence on the Roman Catholic side. He says, "The Germans, who became the largest incoming group after the Civil War, believed that the loss of language was tantamount to the loss of faith. Their emphasis on parochial schools, Catholic press, and social organizations had a strong cultural undertone." See Joseph N. Moody, "A Catholic View of Contemporary Conflict," in Arthur Hertzberg, Martin E. Marty, and Joseph N. Moody, *The Outbursts That Await Us* (New York: The Macmillan Company, 1963), p. 69.

6. James Hastings Nichols, "Religion and Education in a Free Society" in *Religion in America* (*op. cit.*), p. 152.

7. Adolph E. Meyer, *An Educational History of the American People* (New York: McGraw-Hill Book Co., Inc., 1957), p. 162.

8. Horace Mann, *The Republic and the School: The Education of Free Men,* Lawrence A. Cremin, ed. (New York: Bureau of Publications, Teachers College, Columbia University, 1957), p. 92.

9. *Ibid.,* p. 18.

10. Truman M. Post, "A Plea for Western Colleges" in H. Shelton Smith, Robert T. Handy, Lefferts A. Loetscher, *American Christianity* (New York: Charles Scribner's Sons, 1963), II, 50.

11. Sidney E. Mead, *The Lively Experiment* (New York: Harper & Row, Inc., 1963), p. 67.

12. In his illuminating essay Bernard Bailyn warns about the dangers of reading back into earlier times the present-day categories of "public" and "private" education: "The modern conception of public education, the very idea of a clean line of separation beteween 'private' and 'public,' was unknown before the end of the eighteenth century."—*Educa-*

*tion in the Forming of American Society* (New York: Vintage Books, 1960), p. 11.

13. M. B. Cheney, ed., *Life and Letters of Horace Bushnell* (New York: Harper & Brothers, 1880), p. 301.

14. For evidence of what was happening in Bushnell's home state, read George Stewart, *A History of Religious Education in Connecticut to the Middle of the Nineteenth Century* (New Haven: Yale University Press, 1947), pp. 292-293. Cf. Anson Phelps Stokes, *Church and State in the United States* (New York: Harper & Brothers, 1950), I, 409 ff.

15. Sidney E. Mead, *The Lively Experiment* (*op. cit.*), p. 67.

16. Will Herberg, "Religion, Democracy, and Public Education" in *Religion in America,* John Cogley, ed. (*op. cit.*), pp. 128-129. Herberg's statement is helpful because it doubtless requires an observer sensitive to the pressure of an unconscious majority to sense the probable unity-in-diversity of the quarreling Protestant denominations during this period.

17. Cited by Ellwood Cubberley, *Readings in the History of Education* (Boston: Houghton Mifflin Co., 1920), p. 563.

18. Horace Mann, *The Republic and the School: The Education of Free Men,* Lawrence A. Cremin, ed. (*op. cit.*), p. 98.

19. *Ibid.,* p. 100.

20. *Ibid.,* p. 101.

21. George Stewart, *A History of Religious Education in Connecticut to the Middle of the Nineteenth Century* (*op. cit.*), p. 306.

22. Winthrop S. Hudson, *The Great Tradition of the American Churches* (New York: Harper & Brothers, 1953), pp. 150-151.

23. Horace Bushnell, *Christian Nurture* (New Haven: Yale University Press, 1947), p. 60.

24. For confirmation, see H. Clay Trumbull, *The Sunday School: Its Origin, Mission, Methods and Auxiliaries* (New York: Charles Scribner's Sons, 1906), pp. vi-vii.

25. "The church life—that is, the Holy Spirit—collects families into a common organism, and then, by sanctifying the laws of organic unity in families, extends its quickening power to the generation following, so as to include the future, and make it one with the past."—Horace Bushnell, *Christian Nurture* (*op. cit.*), p. 94.

26. Bushnell records with approval a statement made by Jonathan Edwards in his Farewell Sermon, "Every Christian family ought to be, as it were, a little church, consecrated to Christ and wholly influenced and governed by his rules."—*Christian Nurture* (*op. cit.*), p. 159.

I believe, however, that Edwards—and John Calvin before him—was consistent in the interpretation that the family, properly understood, bears the image of the church, whereas Bushnell did not always emphasize the priority of the church as the image of creative community.

27. Horace Bushnell, *Christian Nurture* (*op. cit.*), pp. 144 f.

28. Bushnell developed what I call an "ethos ethic." His use of "nurture" is similar to the manner in which some present-day ethicists employ the word "ethos." For example, see *Christian Nurture* (*op. cit.*), pp. 19-20. A strain of romanticism ran throughout his rhapsodic portrait of the unique environment of the family. Even so, I think that *Christian*

*Nurture* was more than another appeal for family piety or the renewal of the family *per se*. Anne L. Kuhn in her historical survey—*The Mother's Role in Childhood Education: New England Concepts 1830-1860* (New Haven: Yale University Press, 1947)—demonstrates how popular these appeals were during the period when Bushnell was working on *Christian Nurture*. Bushnell's intent was different from that of many of his contemporaries. He was not so concerned with the restoration of the family to its former glory, as he was with the reformation of the church, within which the family plays a crucial role.

29. Winfred E. Garrison probably has Bushnell in mind when he says: "With 90% of the population outside the churches, the task of organized religion could not be limited to encouraging 'Christian nurture' . . . in Christian families, or to ministering to old members as they moved to new places farther west. It had to be directed toward that 90%. What they needed first was not nurture or edification, but radical conversion. . . ."—Cited by Sidney Mead, *The Lively Experiment* (*op. cit.*), p. 122.

30. Winthrop S. Hudson, *The Great Tradition of the American Churches* (*op. cit.*), p. 72.

31. E. Morris Fergusson, *Historic Chapters in Christian Education in America* (Westwood, N. J.: Fleming H. Revell Co., 1935), pp. 39-40. In this respect the Sunday school development was the important precursor of later movements toward interdenominational co-operation and church unity. See the work by H. Shelton Smith, Robert A. Handy, Lefferts A. Loetscher, *American Christianity* (*op. cit.*,), II, 564-565.

32. This sense of rivalry between Sunday school and church lingered on well into the twentieth century. So in the 1930's J. H. Vincent's challenge—"All the Church in the Sunday school, all the Sunday school in the Church"—was still considered daring.—E. Morris Fergusson, *Historic Chapters in Christian Education in America* (*op. cit.*), p. 172.

33. H. Clay Trumbull, *The Sunday School* (*op. cit.*), p. 142. Italics supplied.

34. The Sunday school of that time was not universally greeted with enthusiasm. For a catalogue of complaints (circa the 1880's), see H. Clay Trumbull, *The Sunday School* (*op. cit.*), pp. 149 f. Cf. Lewis J. Sherrill, *Lift Up Your Eyes* (*op. cit.*), p. 51.

## CHAPTER 2.

1. The roster of the founding fathers resembles a list out of "Who's Who" in American education at the turn of the century. See *Proceedings of the First Annual Convention, Chicago, February 10-12, 1903* (Chicago: Religious Education Association, 1903), pp. 340 f.

2. Cited by Orville Davis, "The Religious Education Association," *Orientation in Religious Education,* Philip Henry Lotz, ed. (New York: Abingdon-Cokesbury Press, 1950), p. 445.

3. In this chapter I shall be using the terms "liberal" and "postliberal." These adjectives are slippery words that do not always serve the purpose of precise historical delineation. Both words are employed in these chapters as crude indicators of theological difference. I would define as liberal those educators who were in sympathy with the *theology* of the religious education movement in its evolution from the thought

of George A. Coe in *A Social Theory of Religious Education* (New York: Charles Scribner's Sons, 1917), to the work of Harrison S. Elliott's *Can Religious Education Be Christian?* (New York: The Macmillan Company, 1940). Though these two works vary in emphasis, they are informed by a common "Christ-of-Culture" theological method. See H. Richard Niebuhr, *Christ and Culture* (New York: Harper & Brothers, 1951), pp. 83-115. I employ the term "postliberal" in much the same way as it is ably defined in "The Post-Liberal Theological Mind" in H. Shelton Smith, Robert A. Handy, and Lefferts A. Loetscher, *American Christianity* (New York: Charles Scribner's Sons, 1963), II, 426 f.

4. In the 1930's and 1940's George A. Coe was often referred to as "the Dean of American religious education." Coe was that—and, indeed, something more. He was really the father of the movement. By virtue of his intellectual and moral energy he overshadowed all his coworkers. Some of Coe's most productive years were spent as a professor at Union Seminary (1909-1922). When he resigned from his Union post and moved "across Broadway" to Teachers College, Columbia University, he was succeeded by Harrison S. Elliott (1922-1950). After retirement from Union Theological Seminary, Elliott became executive secretary of the REA. But his death a year later cut short his plans for the rejuvenation of the REA and also the cause of religious education. With the death of Elliott in 1951 the REA took on a different orientation and task, and religious education had lost its last major public spokesman. For all practical purposes, the life of the movement as a major force was over in 1951.

5. Lawrence A. Cremin, *The Transformation of the School* (New York: Alfred A. Knopf, Inc., 1961), p. viii.

6. Adelaide Case, "Christian Education" in *The Church Through Half a Century: Essays in Honor of William Adams Brown,* Samuel M. Cavert and Henry P. Van Dusen, eds. (New York: Charles Scribner's Sons, 1936), p. 233.

7. *Ibid.,* p. 237.

8. *Ibid.,* p. 233.

9. Arlo A. Brown, *A History of Religious Education in Recent Times* (New York: Abingdon-Cokesbury Press, 1923), pp. 80, 81-82.

10. *Ibid.,* p. 195.

11. Adelaide Case, "Christian Education," *The Church Through Half a Century (op. cit.),* p. 233.

12. Winthrop S. Hudson, *The Great Tradition of the American Churches* (New York: Harper & Brothers, 1953), p. 210.

13. J. Coert Rylaarsdam, "The Doctrine of the Church and the Problem of Culture," *Christianity and Society* XVIII (Autumn, 1953), 13. Rylaarsdam's thesis is highly suggestive: "We have already said enough about this to warrant a general statement: when Jewish or Catholic expressions of the Church in its cultural dimensions decay, there is ossification; in Protestantism there is evaporation" (p. 13.).

14. R. Freeman Butts and Lawrence A. Cremin, *A History of Education in American Culture* (New York: Holt, Rinehart & Winston, Inc., 1953), p. 408.

15. For a moving account of a boy's struggle to go to school amidst the pressure of farm life in the nineteenth century, read Hamlin Garland,

*A Son of the Middle Border* (New York: The Macmillan Company, 1917), especially pp. 192 f.

16. R. Freeman Butts and Lawrence A. Cremin, *A History of Education in American Culture* (*op. cit.*), p. 408.

17. *Ibid.* Another index of change was the growth in the number of high schools. In the middle decades of the last century public high schools were still scarce. After 1890 the high school came into its own, and, by the end of World War I, was firmly established as an integral part of the "educational ladder" (*ibid.*), p. 419.

18. Charles H. Thurber, "Religious and Moral Education Through Public and Private Schools," *Proceedings of the First Annual Convention, Chicago, February 10-12, 1903* (*op. cit.*), p. 128. Thurber's further comment about the school's responsibility in moral education is very instructive: "Some children are not reared in moral and religious homes; some do not have the refining and Christianizing influence of the church; but it should be the heritage of every child to be taught by a noble Christian teacher" (p. 147). It was not possible, Thurber admitted, for the school to engage in "sectarian" religious teaching; but at the turn of the century a Protestant could still assume that the "Christian forces" (of a Protestant persuasion) would continue to be safely dominant in school affairs.

19. For a short time during and after World War I, Athearn was accepted as among the more promising of the leaders in the religious education movement. In the late 1920's he was included in a list of the ten most outstanding church educators. See Paul H. Vieth, *Objectives in Religious Education* (New York: Harper & Brothers, 1930), p. 72. For a report on Athearn, see the notice in *Religious Education*, XXX (1930), 6-8.

20. Walter S. Athearn, *Religious Education and American Democracy* (Boston: The Pilgrim's Press, 1917), pp. 60-61. The implication of this statement is more important than the statement itself. He implies that institutional control—and inter-institutional competition—is mediated through the pressure for time. Time becomes an important index of loyalty.

21. *Ibid.*, p. 14. Note how Athearn automatically appeals to the notion of a Protestant parallelism.

22. Walter S. Athearn, *Religious Education and American Democracy* (*op. cit.*), pp. 113-114.

23. The failure of the "Malden Plan" for Malden, Mass., was due to many factors, only one of which is treated in this account.

24. *Ibid.*, p. 49.

25. Walter S. Athearn, *op. cit.*, p. 151. "A community system of religious education must rest upon a *permanent, co-operative religious* organization" (p. 149). This organization was to be the exact counterpart of the public school board.

26. *Ibid.*, p. 154.

27. Athearn's perspective and proposals are similar to the thought of Henry F. Cope as expressed in one of his books, *The Week-Day Church-School* (New York: George H. Doran, 1921).

28. When I state that the Sunday school was the *first* commitment, I do not mean to imply that it was the *only* institutional form of church education. During these years (1900-1935) American Protestantism

had developed other educational activities—as, for instance, the "youth fellowship" in myriad expressions, church-sponsored recreation. Yet these other activities, however important, were usually considered to be in addition to the Sunday school. It was the unspoken assumption (unspoken because it seemed so apparent) that the establishment of a Sunday school was the first task in Protestant church education.

29. George A. Coe, "Discussions of Conference on Week-Day Religious Education," *Religious Education,* XVII (1922), 256.

30. Adelaide Case, "Christian Education" in *The Church Through Half a Century* (*op. cit.*), p. 242.

31. Herbert W. Schneider, *Religion in Twentieth Century America* (Cambridge: Harvard University Press, 1952), p. 38.

32. E. L. Shaver, "How Effective Is Religious Education in Meeting the Present Situation?", *Religious Education,* XXXI (1936), 131.

33. Robert T. Handy, "The American Religious Depression, 1925-1935," *Church History,* XXIX (1960), 3-16.

34. George A. Coe's comment in 1933 is revealing. "All observers," he said, "agree that, in Protestant circles at least, what is called religious education has been losing standing for several years. What its standing actually was at the outset of the present depression is now shown by the way in which churches are meeting the economic strain." See George A. Coe, "The Present Crisis in Religious Education," *Religious Education,* XXVIII (1933), 182.

35. H. Shelton Smith, "Let Religious Educators Reckon with Barthianism," *Religious Education,* XXIX (1934), 45-50.

36. Laird T. Hites, "Religion and Education: Preliminary Statement for the Annual Meeting," *Religious Education,* XXXVI (1941), 66.

37. *Ibid.*

38. Luther A. Weigle, "Public Education and Religion," *Religious Education,* XXXV (1940), 70.

39. *Ibid.,* 69.

40. Mr. Weigle remarked: ". . . the Sunday school movement itself had something to do with the secularization of public education. If we go back to the literature of the 1830's and 1840's, we find that it was the ready recourse of folk, if they were confronted with some question about the taking of religion out of public school education, to turn to the Sunday school. 'We have this new agency,' they would say. 'The Sunday school will train our children in religion.' Henry Barnard played on that string constantly." (*Ibid.,* 70)

41. F. Ernest Johnson, *The Social Gospel Re-Examined* (New York: Harper & Brothers, 1940), pp. 175-176.

42. Later on in the 1940's, Ernest L. Shaver said: "Neither the International Council of Religious Education nor its denominational or state units, with few exceptions, have set out to multiply weekday programs." —"Trends in Weekday Religious Education," *Religious Education,* XLIV (1949), 34.

This practice of niggardly support apparently continued. In 1948 the International Council filed "a friend of the Court" brief before the United States Supreme Court in connection with the McCollum case. Included in that brief was the assertion that ". . . the International Council was organized to promote religious education, principally weekday religious education." But, as Mr. Shaver commented rather bitterly, "The Council showed this *principal* intent by giving less than two per cent of its budget and less than full time of one staff member to it" (*ibid.*).

43. Among its most persistent critics was Conrad H. Moehlman. See, for example, his book, *School and Church: The American Way* (New York: Harper & Brothers, 1944), pp. 131 ff.

44. Cited by Henry P. Van Dusen in *God and Education* (New York: Charles Scribner's Sons, 1951), p. 116. President Van Dusen joined Dean Weigle in upholding the possibilities of teaching a "common core" faith in the public schools.

45. F. Ernest Johnson, *The Social Gospel Re-Examined* (*op. cit.*), p. 187. The same point of view was elaborated more fully in the report of the Committee on Religion and Education (of which Mr. Johnson was the chairman), American Council on Education, *The Relation of Religion to Public Education: The Basic Principles* (American Council on Education Studies, Series I, Reports of Committees and Conferences, No. 26, Vol. XI, April, 1947). Nearly twenty years later this report still ranks as one of the most judicious and intelligent surveys of the problems involved in public school instruction about religious beliefs and institutions.

46. George A. Coe, "The Crux of Our Problem," *Religious Education*, XXXV (1940), 156.

47. In George A. Coe's review of a book by J. Paul Williams, *The New Education and Religion: A Challenge to Secularism in Education* (New York: Association Press, 1945), *Religious Education*, XL, 181-182. Coe embraced wholeheartedly the thesis set forth in Mr. Williams' essay. He spoke of it as ". . . a really fresh approach to the mounting anxiety over the alleged absence of religion from public school education" (p. 180). The argument of this book appears in abbreviated form in some of Mr. Williams' later works. See, for instance, J. Paul Williams, *What Americans Believe and How They Worship:* A Revised Edition (New York: Harper & Row, Inc., 1962), pp. 476 f. For some illuminating comments on the historical significance of Mr. Williams' point of view, see Sidney E. Mead, *The Lively Experiment* (New York: Harper & Row, Inc., 1963), pp. 68-71. Since Coe identified himself so completely with the essential argument advanced by Mr. Williams (which is further corroborated by Coe's fragmentary writings on this subject), much of Mr. Mead's historical interpretation also pertains to to the thought of George A. Coe.

48. George A. Coe, "The Crux of Our Problem," *Religious Education*, XXXV (1940), 157.

49. See Sidney E. Mead, *The Lively Experiment* (*op. cit.*), pp. 68-71.

50. H. Shelton Smith, *Faith and Nurture* (New York: Charles Scribner's Sons, 1942), p. 202.

51. See, for instance, Herbert W. Bashfield, "Extension into Relation with Families," *Religious Education*, XVIII (1923), 116-117, and the articles following; the issue of *Religious Education*, XIX (Apr., 1924); George W. Fiske, "The Religious Task of the Family," *Religious Education*, XXIII (1928), 1014.

52. "The active concern of the home with religious education is our only hope," a lament uttered in the depths of the depression [see an article by Imogene McPherson, "Trends in Parent Education," *Religious*

*Education,* XXVIII (1933), 67], was re-echoed often throughout the decade. The economic crisis contributed force to this sentiment. In the absence of professionally trained personnel, the parents constituted the major source of leadership in parish programs. There were other factors: (1) the apparent success of progressive educators in securing home and day school co-operation (Cf. Adelaide Case, "What May Be Expected of Religious Educators in the Present Scene," *Religious Education,* XXXI (1936), 138, and Abbot Bok, "Making the Home Emphasis Effective," *International Journal of Religious Education,* XI (1934), 9); (2) in a small way, the belated impact of Bushnell's classic, *Christian Nurture* (New Haven; Yale University Press, 1947); (3) the example of Ernest Ligon's emphasis upon the home in his "Character Education Project" at Union College and in neighboring churches; and (4) the growing stream of publications by religious educators on the topic of daily family life. (In 1937, for example, there were three books on this theme, each representing somewhat different perspectives in church education: Regina Westcott Wieman, *The Modern Family and the Church* (New York: Harper & Row, Inc., 1937); Blanche Carrier, *Church Education for Family Life* (New York: Harper & Row, Inc., 1937); Lewis J. Sherrill, *Family and Church* (New York: Abingdon-Cokesbury Press, 1937).

53. International Council of Religious Education, *Christian Education Today* (Chicago: ICRE, 1940), p. 20.

54. *Ibid.*

55. *Ibid.*

56. Later in the 1940's Wesner Fallaw explicitly defined the nature of the church by way of the model of an extended family: "There needs to be the kind of relationship between the family of a child's grandparents and his own immediate family. I have said that the church is people. It should be added that the church ought to be also families— and a *family.*"—Wesner Fallaw, *The Modern Parent and the Teaching Church* (New York: The Macmillan Company, 1946), p. 20. For Fallaw and many fellow educators of that time, the family was the normative mode of association and the prefigurement of true community.

57. Paul H. Vieth, "Christian Education Through the Family," *International Journal of Religious Education,* XV (Oct., 1938), 8.

58. International Council of Religious Education, *Christian Education Today* (*op. cit.*), p. 21.

59. *Ibid.,* pp. 20-21.

60. *Ibid.,* p. 21.

61. "Thus the Church and family serve and support each other, not chiefly from duty or even from choice, but because they have so much in common" (*ibid.,* p. 22).

62. During the 1930's W. E. Ogburn developed his thesis about the transfer of the family's former functions to other institutions in contemporary society. (See, for example, W. E. Ogburn, "The Family and Its Function," *Recent Social Trends in the United States,* Report of the President's Research Committee on Social Trends, 1933.) His argument and the ensuing debate among sociologists over its merits were both based on some common assumptions: (1) The family belongs to a complex network of inter-institutional relationships. The social analysts of that time were thus critical of any tendency to "reify" the family,

to abstract it out of its social setting; (2) The family is often a dependent institution, reflecting changes occurring elsewhere in society.

63. A refreshing exception is George A. Coe, who in his later years developed a quasi-Marxist critique of church education. See his neglected work, *What Religion Is Doing to Our Conscience* (New York: Charles Scribner's Sons, 1943).

64. Lawrence A. Cremin, *The Transformation of the School* (New York: Alfred A. Knopf, Inc., 1961), p. 328.

65. For an excellent study of this venture, see William B. Kennedy, *The Genesis and Development of the Christian Faith and Life Series* (a dissertation presented to the Graduate Faculty of Yale University for the degree of Doctor of Philosophy, 1957).

66. James D. Smart, *The Teaching Ministry of the Church* (Philadelphia: The Westminister Press, 1954), pp. 54-83.

67. Roy W. Fairchild and John Charles Wynn report that by 1958 "... among the Protestant denominations which provide such home-related curriculums are the following: American Baptists, Church of God, Congregational-Christian, Disciples of Christ, Evangelical and Reformed, Lutheran Church—Missouri Synod, Methodist, Protestant Episcopal, Southern Baptist, United Lutheran. . . . Collectively these denominations report about 35 million members."—Roy M. Fairchild and John Charles Wynn, *Families in the Church: A Protestant Survey* (New York: Association Press, 1961), p. 50.

68. William B. Kennedy, *The Genesis and Development of the Christian Faith and Life Series* (*loc. cit.*, Note 65), p. 545.

69. Wesner Fallaw, *Church Education for Tomorrow* (Philadelphia: The Westminister Press, 1960), p. 53.

70. See the excellent analysis by James D. Smart, *The Teaching Ministry of the Church* (*op. cit.*), pp. 187-204.

## CHAPTER 3.

1. H. Richard Niebuhr, "The Protestant Movement and Democracy in the United States" in *The Shaping of American Religion,* James Ward Smith and A. Leland Jamison, eds. (Princeton: Princeton University Press, 1961), p. 47.

2. Engel v. Vitale, June, 1962.

3. Abingdon School District v. Schempp; Murray v. Curlett, June, 1963.

4. Robert S. Gallagher, "God's Little Helpers," *The Reporter,* XXX (June 4, 1964), p. 24.

5. In the ensuing furor over these decisions, it has sometimes been forgotten that only six of the fifty states presently *require* religious exercise in the schools; there are another nine states where prayer or Bible readings are conducted as a matter of tradition in some of the schools. There are, however, twenty-five states that explicitly forbid devotional services, and another ten states where it is not the general practice to engage in these exercises in the classroom. For further information see *U. S. News & World Report,* LVI (May 18, 1964), 63.

6. Reported in *The New York Times,* Sept. 10, 1963. Italics supplied.

7. Peter Schrag, "Searching for Certitudes," *The Commonweal,* LXXIX (Oct. 4, 1963), 37.

8. *Moral and Spiritual Values in the Public Schools* (Washington, D. C.: Educational Policies Commission, National Education Association and

the American Association of School Administrators, (1951), pp. 17-30.

9. Franklin Sherman, "A Lutheran Theological Perspective on the Public Schools," *Religious Education*, LVI (1961), 436.

10. Neil Gerard McCluskey, S. J., *Public Schools and Moral Education* (New York: Columbia University Press, 1958), pp. 260-261.

11. Out of the many possible examples, I would call attention to two influential statements: (1) "The Church and the Public Schools," a statement of the official position of the Presbyterian Church in the U.S.A., adopted by the 169th General Assembly meeting in Omaha, Neb., May 20, 1957, and reported in *Social Progress*, XLVII (July, 1957), 4 f.; (2) "The Churches and the Public Schools," a statement by the General Board of the National Council of the Churches of Christ in the U.S.A., June 7, 1963.

12. Walter Rauschenbusch, *Christianizing the Social Order* (New York: The Macmillan Company, 1912), p. 145.

13. F. Ernest Johnson attempted to fight this general tendency. See, in particular, his fine work, *The Social Gospel Re-Examined* (New York: Harper & Brothers, 1940), pp. 153-191. The topic of public education, he said, ". . . is rarely treated in a book on Christian ethics" (p. 190). Yet even Mr. Johnson confined most of his attention to the particular problems of religion in the public schools.

14. John C. Bennett, *Christians and the State* (New York: Charles Scribner's Sons, 1958), pp. 246-247.

15. James B. Conant, *Education and Liberty: The Role of the Schools in a Modern Democracy* (New York: Vintage Books, 1953), p. 81. For an excellent bibliography of the controversy surrounding this charge, see Edmond G. Drouin, *The School Question: A Bibliography on Church-State Relationships in American Education, 1940-1960* (Washington, D. C.: The Catholic University Press of America, 1963), pp. 227-230.

16. Will Herberg, "Religion, Democracy and Public Education," *Religion in America* (New York: Meridian Press, Inc., 1958), p. 146.

17. *Ibid.*, p. 145.

18. *Ibid.*, p. 146.

19. James B. Conant, *Slums and Suburbs: A Commentary on Schools in Metropolitan Areas* (New York: McGraw-Hill Book Co., Inc., 1961).

20. "The Churches and the Public Schools," A Policy Statement of the National Council of Churches adopted by the General Board on June 7, 1963 in New York City, *International Journal of Religious Education*, XL No. 1 (Sept., 1963), 22.

21. Paul Goodman, *Compulsory Mis-Education* (New York: Horizon Press, 1964), p. 29.

22. Solon T. Kimball and James E. McClellan, Jr., *Education and the New America* (New York: Random House, 1962), p. 91.

23. Christopher Jencks, "Slums and Schools—I," *The New Republic*, CXLVII (Sept. 10, 1962), 19.

24. It is important not to equate productive learning with occupational proficiency. Kimball and McClellan attempt to indicate the fuller dimensions of productive learning ". . . by noting some obvious instances of its absence. A worker whose skills have been rendered obsolete by technological change and who lacks the attitude and motivation (though not the intellectual capacity) for successful retraining somehow failed to learn productively in his school career. So also a housewife whose life becomes drab and meaningless when her children no longer

need her constant attention. So also the citizen who casts his vote according to inherited prejudices rather than following a reasoned appraisal of the alternatives open to him" (*op. cit.,* p. 294).

25. Middle-class parents are apt to pose this question in a simpler form—"Will my child get into college?" It is so easy to lampoon parental anxiety that we sometimes overlook the significance of their queries. One could develop a capsule summary of the changes in American education by comparing the typical questions of parents in different periods: in nineteenth-century America—"Is our child good?"; in the progressive era—"Is he happy and well-adjusted?"; in contemporary times—"Does he know anything" or, more to the point, "Has he learned how to keep learning?"

26. Thus far, the most persuasive arguments in this conversation are those of the advocates of a new kind of intellectuality. Such educators as Kimball and McClellan claim that competence in our world is to be gained through appropriation of the cognitive disciplines, those methods of inquiry taught in the graduate schools and now increasingly available by way of curricular innovation on the elementary and secondary level. The radical character of their claim becomes clear in the following statement: "What relation, then, between an individual world *is* demanded by the world of contemporary metropolitan culture? Clarity, vigor and breadth of thought as discussed under the disciplines of education [earlier described under the rubrics of the displines of logic and mathematics, experimentation, natural history, and esthetic form (*op. cit.,* pp. 298-304)]? These are, of course, essential; without them the world is not, and chaos obtains. But is nothing beyond knowledge necessary? Other social and material worlds have demanded obedience, reverence, devotion. . . . Does our world demand only disciplined thought?

"Not quite. But it doesn't demand any of these other forms of worship. In fact, it makes worship very difficult" (*op. cit.,* p. 308).

27. John R. Seeley, R. Alexander Sim, and Elizabeth W. Loosley, *Crestwood Heights: A Study in Suburban Culture* (New York: Basic Books, Inc., 1956), p. 241.

28. The diagram would be more accurate if the designation, "Teacher," were changed to "School." It is the school as an institution, and not the teacher alone, that makes such a substantial impact upon the parent. Also one should keep in mind the middle-class flavor of the "Crestwood Heights" picture; obviously enough, it would not be equally true of parents in all strata of society.

29. Philip Scharper, "Catholics and the Public Schools," *The Commonweal,* LXXIX (Jan. 31, 1964), 534.

30. There are many other possible descriptive phrases for this plan: split time, reserved time, dual school enrollment, etc. For further information, see Research Report 1964-R10, *Shared-Time Programs: An Exploratory Study* (Research Division, National Education Association, 1964), p. 5.

31. For instance, see John C. Bennett, *Christians and the State* (*op. cit.,*), p. 243.

32. Harry L. Stearns, "Shared Time: Answer to an Impasse," *Christianity and Crisis,* XXI (Sept. 18, 1961), 154.

33. *Ibid.,* p. 157.

34. *Ibid.,* p. 155.

35. See the comment by Paul Vieth in "Shared Time: A Symposium," *Religious Education,* LVII (1962), 34.

36. Leo Pfeffer, *Creeds in Competition: A Creative Force in American Culture* (New York: Harper & Brothers, 1958), p. 70.

37. It has now been three years since Mr. Stearns first put forth his proposal. Yet there have been few—if any—indications of Protestant participation in the new programs of shared time. See, for example, Research Report 1964-R10, *Shared-Time Programs: An Exploratory Study* (*op. cit.*), p. 11-12.

38. George R. LaNoue, *Public Funds for Parochial Schools?* (New York: published for the Department of Religious Liberty, National Council of Churches of Christ in the U. S. A., 1963), p. 45.

39. This judgment of Hugh Douglas Price is cited by Frank J. Munger and Richard F. Fenno, Jr., *National Politics and Federal Aid to Education* (Syracuse: Syracuse University Press, 1962), p. 171.

40. In advancing this speculation, I am neither condoning nor condemning such a possible "solution." The legal and social problems surrounding the issue of federal aid to education are far too complex to be treated adequately within the brief confines of this essay.

41. John C. Bennett, *Christians and the State* (*op. cit.*), p. 244.

42. Dean M. Kelley, "Protestants and Parochial Schools," *The Commonweal,* LXXIX (Jan. 31, 1964), 521-522.

43. There are two other conditions that might encourage the development of Protestant day schools: the fear of Catholic domination in school affairs, and the deterioration of an urban school system. Yet I doubt that either one of these circumstances would impel many Protestants to pay the costs (moral and financial) of establishing day schools. A less expensive (though equally irresponsible) solution is mobility.

44. For an illuminating comment on this problem see Robert T. Francoeur, "The Price We Pay," *The Commonweal,* LXXIX (Jan. 31, 1964), 538-542.

## CHAPTER 4.

1. Cited by Lionel Trilling, *The Liberal Imagination* (New York: The Viking Press, 1950), p. 6.

2. H. Shelton Smith, *Faith and Nurture* (New York: Charles Scribner's Sons, 1942), p. ix.

3. James D. Smart, *The Creed in Christian Teaching* (Philadelphia: The Westminster Press, 1962), p. 8.

4. "Shall We Pray," *The New Republic,* CXLVIII (June 29, 1963), 5.

5. Lawrence T. Cremin, *The Transformation of the School* (New York: Alfred A. Knopf, Inc., 1961), p. 350.

6. The proponents of shared time are inclined to press the advantages of this scheme without thinking clearly about its consequences as an educational policy. There are countless questions that come to mind once one sees shared time in relation to other issues. How would its enactment affect the process of desegregation? Would it reinforce the power of the neighborhood school? These questions need to be asked, lest shared time—now viewed as a possible resolution of a church-state matter—be used by local communities as a way of disguising other motives that are not so well-intentioned.

7. "A court is not qualified to order large-scale bussing to distant areas; it is not qualified to decide that the neighborhood system should be

abandoned, or that the so-called Princeton plan of consolidating several grades from a number of neighborhoods in one school can be suitably applied; it is not qualified to estimate the tipping point at which a desegregated school will resegregate—and such judgments will not, and ought not, be accepted from a court."—Alexander M. Bickel, "Beyond Tokenism: The Civil Rights Task That Looms Ahead," *The New Republic,* CL (Jan. 4, 1964), 14.

8. Harlem Youth Opportunities, Inc., *Youth in the Ghetto: A Study of the Consequences of Powerlessness and a Blueprint for Change* (New York: HARYOU, 1964), p. 426.

9. William Lee Miller, "Aid to Education: A Better Deal," *The Reporter,* XXX (Apr. 23, 1964), 20.

10. There is evidence that this search has already commenced. One hopeful sign of change is indicated in the testimony of a spokesman for mainline Protestantism before a Congressional committee in Jan., 1965. After years of hesitation and opposition Protestant leaders are now clearly moving toward accepting a wider range of federal benefits for the child in the parochial school. Such a willingness to venture beyond previous positions may mark the beginning of a new chapter in the history of the Protestant-Catholic debate over aid to education. For further information see Robert W. Lynn, "New Opportunity in Education," *Christianity and Crisis,* XXV (March 8, 1965), 30-31.

11. George R. LaNoue, *Public Funds for Parochial Schools?* (New York: Dept. of Religious Liberty, National Council of Churches, 1963), p. 36.

12. Edgar Z. Friedenberg, *The Vanishing Adolescent* (New York: Dell Publishing Co., 1959), p. 80.

13. *Ibid.,* p. 88.

14. Dean M. Kelley, "Protestants and Parochial Schools," *The Commonweal* LXXIX (Jan. 31, 1964), 522-523.

15. "In ten states with a concentrated Catholic population, Catholic schools now educate between 20 and 25 per cent of the total school enrollment. These schools take an even larger share of the school-going population in certain eastern and midwestern cities: in Dubuque, 61 per cent; in Manchester, 52 per cent; in Pittsburgh, 42 per cent; in Philadelphia, 39 per cent; in Buffalo, 38 per cent; in New Orleans, Milwaukee, and Chicago, 33 per cent; in Cleveland and New York, 26 per cent; in St. Louis, 25 per cent; and in Detroit, 23 per cent."—Neil Gerard Mc-Cluskey, S. J., *Catholic Education in America: A Documentary History* (New York: Bureau of Publications, Teachers College, Columbia University, 1964), pp. 1-2.

16. Arthur Gilbert, "American Public Education and the Challenge of Religious Pluralism" (a talk at an Institute on Religion and the Public Schools, Lafayette, Ind. Oct. 6-9, 1963; mimeographed), p. 10.

17. Wesley Shrader, "Our Troubled Sunday Schools," *Life,* XLII (Feb. 11, 1957), 110-114.

18. Daniel Callahan, "Into the Briar Patch," *The Commonweal,* LXXIX (Jan. 31, 1964), 503.

19. A hopeful beginning in this direction is indicated in the pronouncement, "Federal Aid to Education: The Shared-Time Concept," a statement adopted by the 176th General Assembly of the United Presbyterian Church in the United States of America, Oklahoma City, Okla., May 26, 1964.